Masters: Porcelain

PIET STOCKMANS ■ RUTH DUCKWORTH
■ SUK-YOUNG KANG ■ ANN LINNEMANN ■
ILONA ROMULE ■ JANET DEBOOS ■ REBECCA HARVEY
■ SERGEI ISUPOV ■ YIKYUNG KIM ■ LES LAWRENCE ■
BODIL MANZ ■ ANDREW MARTIN ■ PAUL MATHIEU
■ CHRISTOPHER P. STALEY ■ RICHARD SHAW ■
SUSAN BEINER ■ CURTIS BENZLE ■ PHILIP CORNELIUS
■ CLAIRE CURNEEN ■ PAUL A. DRESANG ■

HARLAN HOUSE ■ LEAH LEITSON ■ KEISUKE MIZUNO ■ SUNKOO YUH ■ EDMUND DE WAAL ■ GWYN HANSSEN PIGOTT ■ KIM SOO-JEONG ■ MATTHEW METZ ■ AYSHA PELTZ ■ LINDA SIKORA ■ KURT WEISER ■ EDWARD S. EBERLE ■ SILVIE GRANATELLI ■ NICHOLAS HOMOKY ■ TAIZO KURODA ■ PRUE VENABLES ■ ARNE ÅSE ■ SANDRA BLACK ■ SAM CHUNG ■ DIANE KENNEY

Masters: Porcelain

Major Works by Leading Ceramists

Curated by Richard Burkett

LARK BOOKS

A Division of Sterling Publishing Co., Inc.
New York / London

EDITOR:
Suzanne J. E. Tourtillott

ART DIRECTOR:
Kathleen Holmes

COVER DESIGNER:
Cindy LaBreacht

ASSISTANT EDITOR:
Shannon Quinn-Tucker

COVER, FAR LEFT:
Sergei Isupov
Sacrifice, 2002
Photo by Katherine Wetzel

COVER, LEFT CENTER:
Keisuke Mizuno
Forbidden Fruit, 1999
Photo by Craig Smith

COVER, CENTER:
Silvie Granatelli
Wavy Edge Dinnerware, 2006
Photo by Molly Selznick

COVER, RIGHT CENTER:
Harlan House
Champagne Meiping, 2001
Photo by artist

COVER, FAR RIGHT:
Richard Shaw
The Painter, 2003
Photo by Charles Kennard

SPINE:
Keisuke Mizuno
Forbidden Flower, 2000
Photo by Anthony Cuñha

BACK COVER, LEFT:
Sunkoo Yuh
Sacrifice, 2005
Photo by Larry Dean

BACK COVER, CENTER:
Gwyn Hanssen Pigott
Still Life with Two Tall Beakers, 2004
Photo by Brian Hand

BACK COVER, RIGHT:
Kurt Weiser
Chihuahua, 2002
Photo by artist

Library of Congress Cataloging-in-Publication Data

Tourtillott, Suzanne J. E.
  Masters--porcelain : major works by leading ceramists / Suzanne J.E. Tourtillott. -- 1st ed.
    p. cm.
  Includes index.
  ISBN-13: 978-1-57990-972-7 (pb-with flaps : alk. paper)
  ISBN-10: 1-57990-972-8 (pb-with flaps : alk. paper)
  1. Porcelain--History--20th century. 2. Porcelain--History--21st century.
  I. Title.
  NK4370.T68 2008
  738.209'051— dc22
                                     2007019765
10 9 8 7 6 5 4 3 2 1

First Edition

Published by Lark Books, A Division of
Sterling Publishing Co., Inc.
387 Park Avenue South, New York, N.Y. 10016

Distributed in Canada by Sterling Publishing,
c/o Canadian Manda Group, 165 Dufferin Street
Toronto, Ontario, Canada M6K 3H6

Distributed in the United Kingdom by GMC Distribution Services,
Castle Place, 166 High Street, Lewes, East Sussex, England BN7 1XU

Distributed in Australia by Capricorn Link (Australia) Pty Ltd.,
P.O. Box 704, Windsor, NSW 2756 Australia

If you have questions or comments about this book, please contact:
Lark Books
67 Broadway
Asheville, NC 28801
(828) 253-0467

Manufactured in China

ISBN 13: 978-1-57990-972-7
ISBN 10: 1-57990-972-8

For information about custom editions, special sales, premium and corporate purchases, please contact Sterling Special Sales Department at 800-805-5489 or specialsales@sterlingpub.com.

Contents

Introduction

PORCELAIN: MASTER WORKS by Leading Ceramists presents an overview of superior artistic ceramic practice by showcasing the work of 40 outstanding creators—sculptors and potters alike—who use porcelain. This book is a fascinating snapshot of porcelain's unique expressive and technical qualities, as well as a glimpse into the thoughts and feelings of the artists who mine its tremendous potential.

Curator and ceramist Richard Burkett, of San Diego State University, invited ceramists from around the globe to contribute images to this, the first in a major new series about some of the top practitioners in fine craft. True, Burkett's choices condense these artists' achievements to a relative mere handful of remarkable pieces—something of a mini-retrospective in print—yet they masterfully illustrate what is unique and worthy of study about such work. Each artist is introduced with a brief statement drawn from both the artist's own words and from Richard Burkett's astute observations on the artist's work as a whole, with particular and poetic attention to the nuances and themes that had initially convinced him of that ceramist's need to be included here. The first thing apparent is that these modern practitioners expand and challenge traditional perceptions of what the medium can—and should—do. Porcelain has always been prized for its unique qualities of pristine whiteness, strength, texture, and even for its resonance. Not quite like any other ceramic material,

porcelain in the right hands is capable of being awesomely delicate as well as expressively forceful. In the 18th century, porcelain attracted the admiration and greed of alchemists and princes; Europeans worked tirelessly to invent a sort of doppelganger that could be made to imitate those precious porcelain pieces the Chinese had first created. For at least some of the artists in this book, that age-old mystique still clings to this unusual and notoriously difficult clay whose very definition remains subject to debate.

These collected works represent the great diversity, both technical and aesthetic, that porcelain affords those ceramists who respond to its siren call. Through personal observation and anecdote, each artist addresses aspects of his or her approach: why this material, why that form, why these private concerns? Some relate early, seminal experiences; others refer to the means and methods that are their current passion or guiding force. Such glimpses and insights take us back to the work with renewed appreciation—and more questions.

A few of the ceramists declare that porcelain's appeal is simply as a convenient and ready source of ideal texture or surface; others claim it affords much more: porcelain as grail, as ideal. Porcelain may be a "perfect" canvas as much as it is the stuff of "perfect" form, yet no creed can knit these 40 artists together too tightly.

Whether functionally referential, quietly meditative, or something else altogether, such diverse works offer a rare look at how modern studio practice can overlap, separate, and yet ultimately flow together more or less harmoniously. Christopher P. Staley thrusts porcelain's materiality to the fore, while some of the fluttering, undulating vessels of Aysha Peltz and Kim Soo-Jeong challenge modernism's core tenet about form serving function. Piet Stockman's and Prue Venables' pieces take the notion a few steps further; they have become a sort of playground on which to tweak the noble nose of function itself.

Richard Shaw keeps his sleight-of-hand realism lighthearted—perhaps in honor of the material's primacy—while Paul Dresang invests his trompe-l'oeil sculptures with darker ruminations. The work of Ilona Romule has a vigorous physicality that stands in confident, easy contrast to more formal and private tales by sculptor-cum-surrealist Sergei Isupov.

Leah Leitson's vessels seem to fairly leap away from gravity's bonds, while Linda Sikora's and Matthew Metz's defer to them by making gorgeous commentaries on the vernacular of the vessel. Ann Linnemann's pots, freed from function altogether, morph into bodily casements while the quietude of Taizo Kuroda pieces exude a nearly human presence. Andrew Martin makes delicate yet witty vessel-sculptures. The bristling sculptural constructions of Susan Beiner reference 18th-century Nymphenburg and other European porcelain objets d'art. Keisuke Mizuno's remarkable sculptures address the life cycle itself. Diversity, we hardly knew ye.

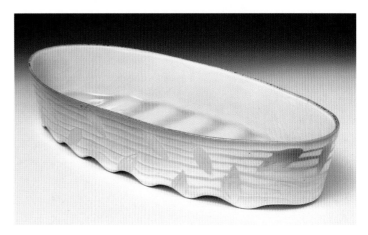

▲ Richard Burkett
Wave Oval | 2006
2½ x 14 x 7 inches (6.4 x 35.6 x 17.8 cm)
Slip cast porcelain, soda fired with shellac-resist decoration and celadon glaze inside
Photo by artist

Present-day artistic studio practice seems to bear little resemblance to the time-honored position of master (or mistress, for that matter), yet there will always be masterful work to admire, discuss, and yes, even emulate. We admit forthrightly and without apology that this book includes only 40 of the very best porcelain artists today. But these unbearably beautiful works deserve your undivided attention.

—Suzanne J. E. Tourtilliott
Editor

Piet Stockmans

CLEARLY INFLUENCED BY the issues of contemporary art—especially those of Europe—Piet Stockmans makes work from porcelain that transcends the pottery traditions that bind many other makers. Yet he often uses and references the process of making ceramics: glaze tests, multiples, and series, including the intense blue and white glazes that are ever popular in the commercial market. Stockmans creates porcelain in very industrial ways, but with humor and innocence that belies the art's underlying seriousness. His use of multiple images can transform a space—occasionally overwhelming the viewer with the sheer multitude of pieces.

◀ **Untitled** │ 2006
18¼ x 1½ inches (46 x 4 cm)
Slip-cast porcelain; glaze;
2570°F (1410°C)
Photo by artist

◀ **Be Mindful, O Man, That Thou Are But Dust and to Porcelain Shalt Thou Return!** | 1994

98½ x 197 feet
(30 x 60 m)
Slip-cast porcelain;
glaze; gas fired, cone 12
Photos by E. van Sloun and
G. Ramaekers

" For me, creation is the result of activity and not of thinking. It is activity that generates ideas, which themselves give rise to other ones, a process during which decisive choices are made in a mysterious way. "

◀ **1,000 Crucibles** | 1980
Each: 1¼ x 1¼ inches
(3.2 x 3.2 cm)
Slip-cast porcelain; glaze;
gas fired, cone 12
Photo by Walter Rawoens

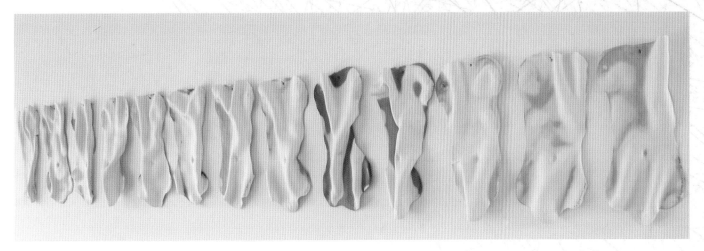

▲ **Human Skin** │ 2006

19¾ x 19¾ x 2 inches (500 x 50.2 x 5.1 cm)

Slip-cast porcelain; unglazed; gas fired, cone 12

Photo by artist

Painted Vases │ 1991 ▶

118 x 118 x 8 inches (300 x 300 x 20.3 cm)

Slip-cast porcelain; unglazed; gas fired, cone 12

Photo by artist

" Ceramists understandably tend to fall in love with their material. They go down on their knees for a nice glaze, a special clay, or an oven they made themselves. However, being in love makes you blind. "

◄ **Boxes with Porcelain Plates** │ 1991
118 x 11¾ x 118 inches
(300 x 30 x 300 cm)
Slip-cast porcelain; unglazed,
gas fired, cone 12
Photo by artist

▲ **Untitled** | 2006

15¾ x 15¾ x 1⅝ inches
(40 x 40 x 4 cm)
Slip-cast porcelain; glaze;
2570°F (1410°C)
Photo by artist

◀ **The Five Human Races** | 2002

3¼ x 15 inches (8.3 x 38.1 cm)
Slip-cast porcelain; unglazed; gas
fired, cone 12
Photo by Walter Rawoens

◀ **Well Installation** │ 1988

118 x 393½ inches
(300 x 1000 cm)
Slip-cast porcelain; unglazed;
gas fired, cone 12
Photo by artist

◀ **Teapot and Concrete** │ 1975

8 x 8 x 8 inches
(20.3 x 20.3 x 20.3 cm)
Slip-cast porcelain; glaze; gas fired,
cone 12
Photo by Walter Rawoens

Folded-Out Vase | 2001 ▶

12½ x 9¾ x 2 inches
(31.8 x 24.8 x 5.1 cm)
Slip-cast porcelain; unglazed;
gas fired, cone 12
Photo by Garth Clark Gallery

▼ **100 Dishes** | 1999

157½ x 472½ inches
(400 x 1200 x 20.3 cm)
Slip-cast porcelain
Photo by Walter Rawoens

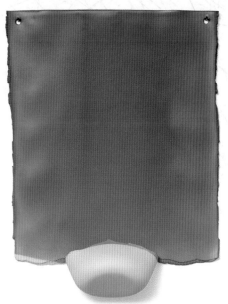

" Clay, glaze, oven, and potter's wheel do not mean anything on their own; they are just aids to express our emotions. To be expressive, this dead material has to be loaded with love, happiness, and a little sadness. "

Ruth Duckworth

NO SURVEY OF CONTEMPORARY porcelain should be without homage to Ruth Duckworth. She has spent a lifetime making sculpture from clay, working primarily in porcelain. Her sculptural work ranges from large, technically challenging forms (often wall-mounted) to small, delicate vessels. Ever the abstractionist, Duckworth occasionally ventures into somewhat more figurative works, but at her best, her work is pure abstraction: formal, elegant, silent.

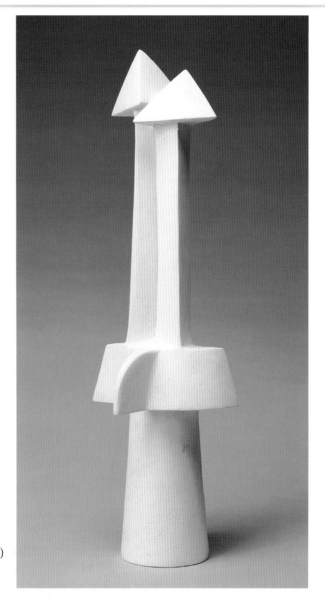

Untitled | 2004 ▶

22 x 7 x 4½ inches
(55.9 x 17.8 x 11.4 cm)
Porcelain
Photo by James Prinz

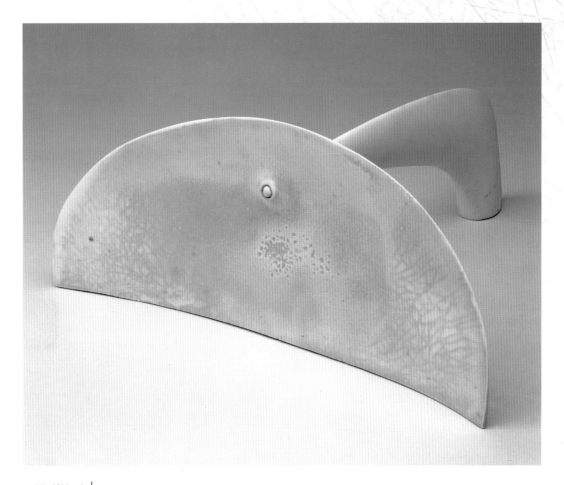

▲ **Untitled** │ 1990

5⅞ x 13½ x 12 inches
(14.9 x 34.3 x 30.5 cm)
Porcelain
Photo by James Prinz

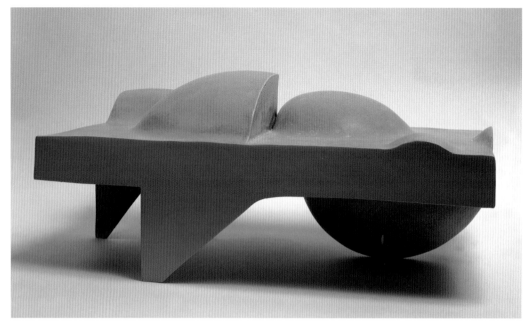

Untitled | 1993 ▶

   8½ x 19¾ x 10 inches
   (21.6 x 50.2 x 25.4 cm)
   Porcelain
   Photo by James Prinz

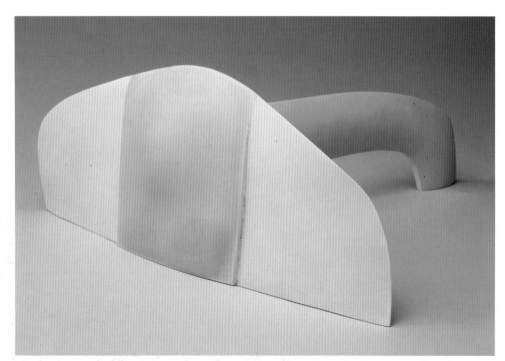

◀ **Untitled** | 1991

   6 x 14½ x 13½ inches
   (15.2 x 36.8 x 34.3 cm)
   Porcelain
   Photo by James Prinz

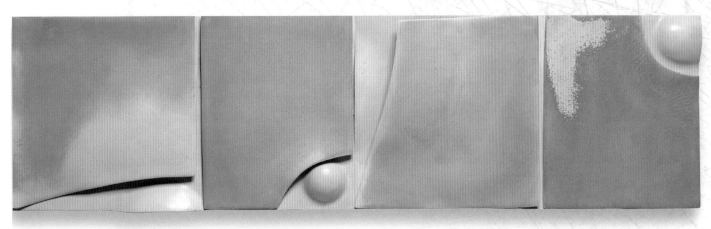

▲ **Untitled** | 2006
18½ x 66¼ x 2½ inches
(47 x 168.3 x 6.4 cm)
Porcelain
Photo by James Prinz

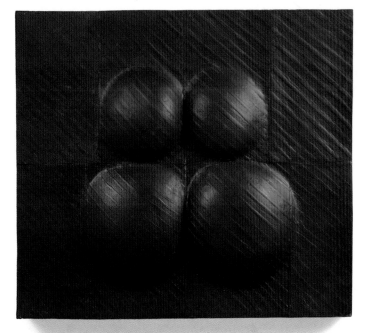

Untitled | 2002 ▶
37 x 42 x 6½ inches
(94 x 106.7 x 16.5 cm)
Porcelain
Photo by James Prinz

" I was a stone carver
for about 13 years
before deciding to
study ceramics. I had
worked with clay, but
knew nothing of glazes
and firings. In my
mind, I was a sculptor
who simply decided to
change mediums.**"**

▲ **Untitled** | 2003
Left: 6½ x 9 x 5½ inches (16.5 x 22.9 x 14 cm);
middle: 9 x 6½ x 3 inches (22.9 x 16.5 x 7.6 cm);
right: 6½ x 9 x 5½ inches (16.5 x 22.9 x 14 cm)
Porcelain
Photo by James Prinz

" Back when I studied ceramics in England, there were rigid requirements and limitations for a ceramic artist. Each piece was to have a foot, a middle, and a lip. As I didn't think about my work in this way, I began creating pieces just like I wanted instead. I didn't think about those rules. "

_____

▲ **Untitled** │ 2005
18¼ x 30¼ x 5 inches (46.4 x 76.8 x 12.7 cm)
Porcelain
Photo by James Prinz

▲ **Untitled** │ 2002
20½ x 21 x 5½ inches (52.1 x 53.3 x 14 cm)
Porcelain
Photo by James Prinz

" Today, many years later, I create my pieces with the same process I've always used. I think of myself still as a sculptor. If you look at my pieces, you will see that every piece I have ever created could possibly be done in clay, bronze, or stone. I don't think of the medium of clay as a limitation—I just like the feel of it, the challenge of it, and the beauty of it. Thus, I work with clay. "

Untitled │ 2006 ▶
37¼ x 38¾ x 8¾ inches
(81.9 x 98.4 x 22.2 cm)
Porcelain
Photo by James Prinz

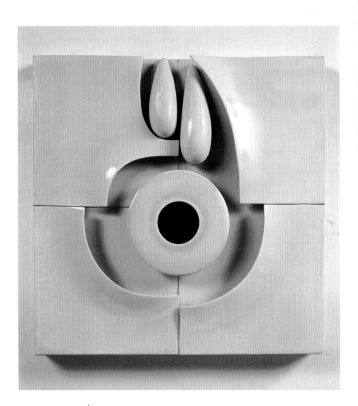

▲ **Untitled** | 2002

31½ x 30 x 8 inches (80 x 76.2 x 20.3 cm)
Porcelain
Photo by James Prinz

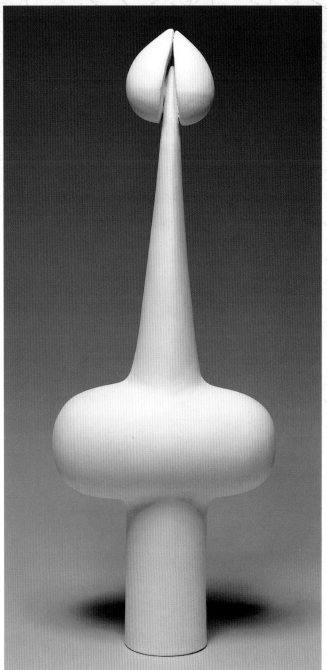

Untitled | 2005 ▶

22 x 7 x 4½ inches
(55.9 x 17.8 x 11.4 cm)
Porcelain
Photo by James Prinz

Suk-Young Kang

THE BEAUTIFULLY ABSTRACT slip-cast work in porcelain by Suk-Young Kang is often geometric in form, but almost always altered to soften the porcelain's stiffness after it comes out of the mold. Often these alterations are gestural, like capturing a frozen action: a punch, a slash, a slump, or a splash of slip. His best work captures the pure white beauty of porcelain by using light and shadow to model the forms. Certain examples of his larger sculptural installations evoke images from nature.

◀ **Untitled** | 2004

12 x 91½ inches (30.5 x 232.4 cm)
Slip-cast porcelain; unglazed; gas fired
Photo by artist

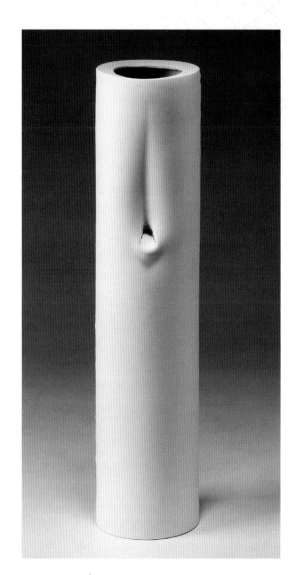

▲ **Untitled** | 1992

   5½ x 24½ inches (14 x 62 cm)
   Slip-cast porcelain; unglazed; gas fired
   Photo by artist

▲ **Untitled** | 2006

   13⅜ x 21¼ inches (34 x 54 cm)
   Slip-cast porcelain; unglazed; gas fired
   Photo by artist

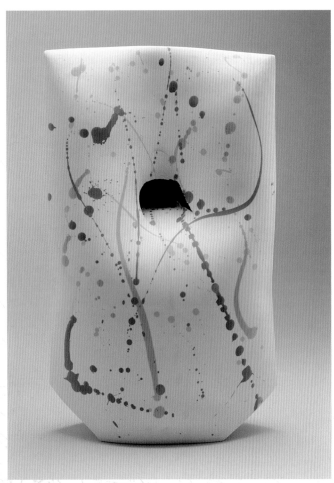

▲ **Untitled** │ 1990

34 x 10 x 49 inches (86.4 x 25.4 x 124.5 cm)
Slip-cast porcelain; unglazed; gas fired
Photo by artist

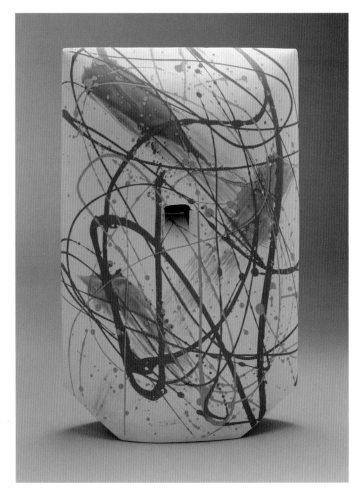

▲ **Untitled** │ 1990

34 x 10 x 49 inches (86.4 x 25.4 x 124.5 cm)
Slip-cast porcelain; unglazed; gas fired
Photo by artist

" My expressions are disciplined interpretations of primitive shapes, depicting a human being emptied of any greed and focusing on the essence of purity and innocence. "

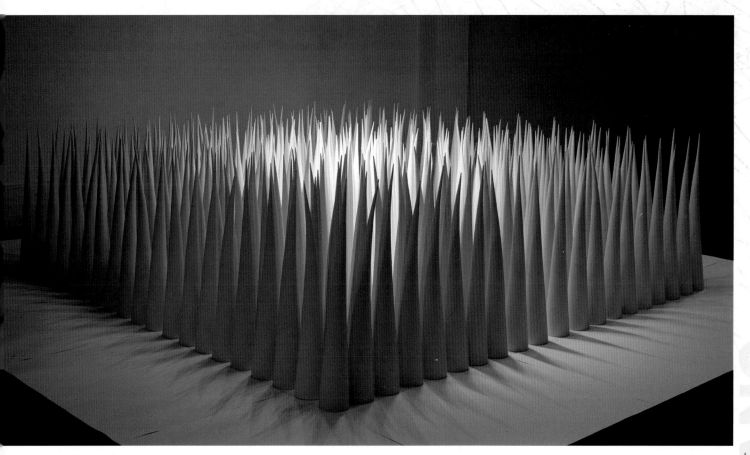

▲ **Untitled** | 2004
   13 x 90 inches (33 x 228.6 cm)
   Slip-cast porcelain; unglazed; gas fired
   Photo by artist

" My work relates to the discipline found in nature, and I am particularly interested in making formations with natural aestheticism. I use white clay bodies and experiment with the different shades of white that result from differences in the application of ceramic ingredients and firing techniques. I am more interested in the naturalness of form created through numerous experimentations than in immaculate technique. "

◀ **Untitled** │ 1997
21 x 19 x 63½ inches
(53.3 x 48.3 x 161.3 cm)
Slip-cast porcelain; unglazed; gas fired
Photo by artist

▲ **Untitled** │ 2000

14¾ x 21 inches (37 x 53 cm)
Slip-cast porcelain; unglazed; gas fired
Photo by artist

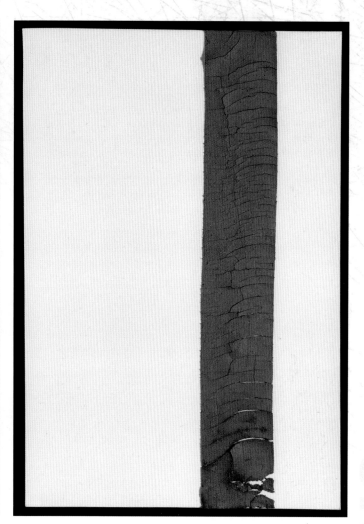

▲ **Untitled** │ 2000

21¾ x 14¾ inches (55 x 37.5 cm)
Slip-cast porcelain; unglazed; gas fired
Photo by artist

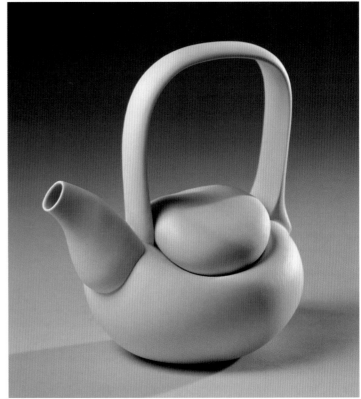

▲ **Untitled** | 2003
  20 x 16 x 24 inches (50.8 x 40.6 x 61 cm)
  Slip-cast porcelain; unglazed; gas fired
  Photo by artist

◄ **Untitled** | 1992
  16½ x 16½ x 66½ inches
  (41.9 x 41.9 x 168.9 cm)
  Slip-cast porcelain; unglazed; gas fired
  Photo by artist

" An important factor in my work is the use of light. The forms are sometimes made in association with lighting. Stressing whiteness is definitely important because different tones in the white can be achieved with lighting. **"**

Untitled | 1995 ▶

33½ x 56 inches (85.1 x 142.2 cm)
Slip-cast porcelain; unglazed; gas fired
Photo by artist

SUK-YOUNG **KANG**

Ann Linnemann

THE BEST OF ANN LINNEMANN'S work questions the ephemeral nature of life. The sensuous surfaces of the abstracted body sections made from porcelain are intriguing. Their insubstantial quality and delicate whiteness (sometimes patterned lightly, as if clothed) suggest mere skin. The soft curves of her other vessels, while not as explicit as the torsos, also exude a corporeal quality. Though thrown initially, it is Linnemann's subtle manipulation of the thin porcelain, adding a bump here, a dent there, that makes these pieces come alive.

◀ **Wine Pot** | 1996

7⅞ x 7⅞ inches (20 x 20 cm)
Thrown and altered porcelain; cut;
unglazed; electric fired, cone 10
Photo by Ole Akhøj

" My sculptural forms,
embodied with elements
of human movement and
body language, reference my
fascination with different
cultures as well as the mind."

◀ **Body Forms** │ 2004–2005
15¾ x 13¾ inches (40 x 35 cm)
Thrown and altered porcelain;
unglazed; wood fired, cone 12;
electric fired, cone 9
Photo by Ole Akhøj

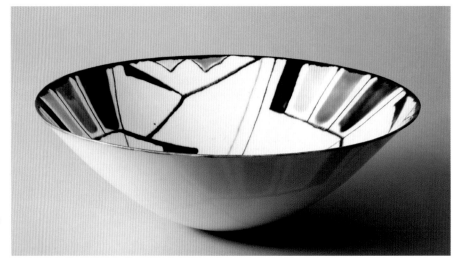

Bowls, Shell Form | 1989 ▶

9¾ x 17¾ inches (24.8 x 45.1 cm)
Slip-cast bone china porcelain; glaze
decoration; electric fired, cone 10
Photo by Ole Akhøj

◀ **Hand Form** | 2001

3½ x 6¼ inches (9 x 16 cm)
Thrown and altered porcelain;
unglazed; electric fired, cone 9
Photo by artist

> *" Most of my pieces are inspired by the human form. They may be laid down or stood up individually, or even connected. "*

▲ **Bowls** | 1996

Each: 4¾ x 4¾ inches (12 x 12 cm)
Thrown and altered porcelain; cut;
unglazed; electric fired, cone 10
Photo by Ole Akhøj

Coffee Pot | 1996 ▶

9⅞ x 9⅞ x 6 inches (25 x 25 x 15 cm)
Thrown and altered porcelain; cut; glaze;
electric fired, cone 10
Photo by Ole Akhøj

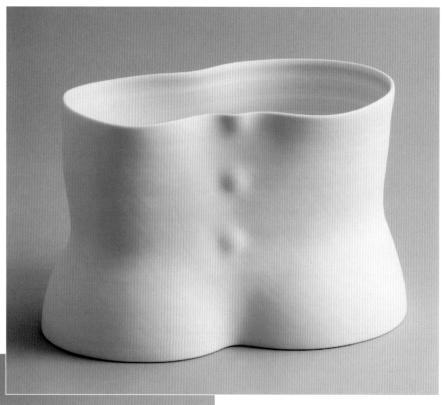

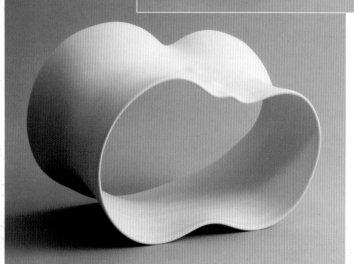

▲ **Body Form** │ 2004

15¾ x 15¾ inches (40 x 40 cm)
Thrown and altered porcelain;
unglazed; electric fired, cone 9
Photos by Ole Akhøj

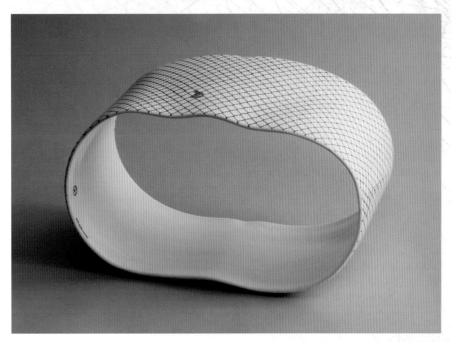

Body Blue | 2004 ▲

13¾ x 17¾ x 11¾ inches
(35 x 45 x 30 cm)
Thrown and altered porcelain; glaze;
blue print; electric fired, cone 9
Photo by Ole Akhøj
Made in collaboration with
Paul Scott, UK (vitrified print)

Body Form | 2005 ▶

13¾ x 15¾ inches (35 x 40 cm)
Thrown and altered porcelain; cut;
unglazed; electric fired, cone 9
Photo by Ole Akhøj

 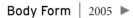

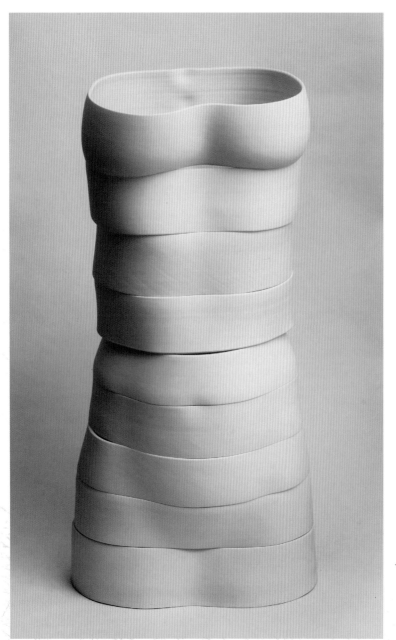

" The naked ceramic form, with its intimate bodily suggestions, is gently shown in pure white porcelain. Settled ashes from the wood-fired kiln dramatically color and accentuate the sculptural forms. "

◄ **Body–Torso III** │ 2005

31½ x 19¾ x 11¾ inches (80 x 50 x 30 cm)
Thrown and altered porcelain; cut; unglazed;
electric fired, cone 9
Photo by Ole Akhøj

▲ **Body** | 2006

16½ x 17¾ x 7⅞ inches (42 x 45 x 20 cm)
Thrown and altered porcelain; unglazed;
wood fired, cone 12
Photo by Ole Akhøj

◀ **Body** | 2006

16½ x 17¾ x 8 inches (42 x 45 x 20 cm)
Thrown and altered porcelain; unglazed;
wood fired, cone 12
Photos by Ole Akhøj

ANN LINNEMANN

Ilona Romule

THE PLAYFULLY QUIRKY porcelain sculptures by Ilona Romule at first disarm the viewer by using animal and human forms, but a closer look reveals much more complexity. From the drawings that cover the surfaces of her pieces to the more overtly sexual elements, Romule's wares feature an otherworldly blend of part-human, part-animal creatures from some futuristic narrative, all in suggestive poses. The cold whiteness and smooth surface of the porcelain contribute important qualities as well.

◀ **The Games of Chameleons,** | 2000
Left: 7½ x 8¾ x 7⅞ inches
(19 x 22 x 20 cm);
Right: 7⅛ x 14¼ x 5⅛ inches
(18 x 36 x 13 cm)
Slip-cast porcelain; glazed interior;
electric fired, cone 10; polished; china
paints and gold luster, cone 018; cork
Photos by artist

▲ **Brutto, Brutto Anatroccolo** | 2005

Teapot: 12¼ x 14½ x 6¼ inches (31 x 37 x 16 cm);
cup: 4 x 6¾ x 3⅛ inches (10 x 17 x 8 cm)
Slip-cast porcelain; green Korean celadon glaze; gas fired in
reduction, cone 11; china paints and luster, cone 018
Photo by artist

" The primary function of figurative porcelain is not as a pot, a bowl, or a cup. I expect viewers to see not just containers for liquid, but containers that hold ideas, emotions, pain, and sexuality.**"**

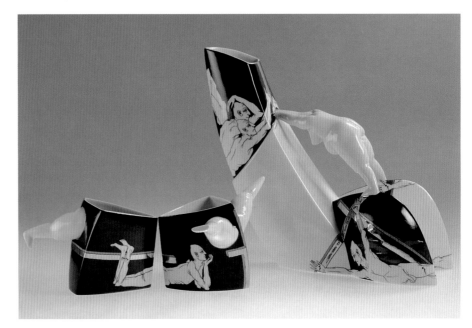

▲ **Everybody Bears His Own Cross** │ 1993

Jug: 11 x 13 x 5½ inches (28 x 33 x 14 cm);
cup: 4¼ x 7⅛ x 3½ inches (11 x 18 x 9 cm)
Slip-cast porcelain; glaze; reduction fired in gas tunnel kiln, cone 11; china paints and gold luster, cone 018
Photo by artist

◀ **Male and Female Candle Holders** │ 1994

Male: 7⅞ x 4¾ x 3½ inches
(20 x 12 x 9 cm);
female: 5 ⅛ x 6 x 3½ inches
(13 x 15 x 9 cm)
Slip-cast porcelain; glaze; electric fired, cone 10; china paints and gold luster, cone 018
Photo by artist

Female Bowls | 1995 ▲

7⅞ x 5½ x 4 inches
(20 x 14 x 10 cm)
Slip-cast porcelain; stained porcelain body (black piece); glaze;
unglazed, polished after firing; gas
fired in reduction, cone 11; china
paints and gold luster, cone 018
Photo by artist

For You | 1995 ▶

Sculpture: 5½ x 14¼ x 5¾ inches
(14 x 36 x 14.5 cm);
bowl: 5½ x 4 ¾ x 3⅛ inches
(14 x 12 x 8 cm)
Slip-cast porcelain; partially glazed;
gas fired in reduction, cone 11;
polished; platinum luster, cone 018
Photo by artist

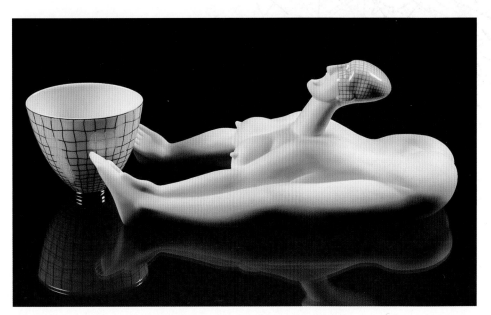

◀ **Bald But Beautiful** | 1999

First pot: 7⅞ x 4 x 4¾ inches
(20 x 10 x 12 cm);
second pot: 10⅝ x 8¼ x 4¾ inches
(27 x 21 x 12 cm)
Slip-cast porcelain; glazed interior;
electric fired, cone 10; polished;
china paints, cone 018; gold luster,
cone 018; cork
Photo by artist

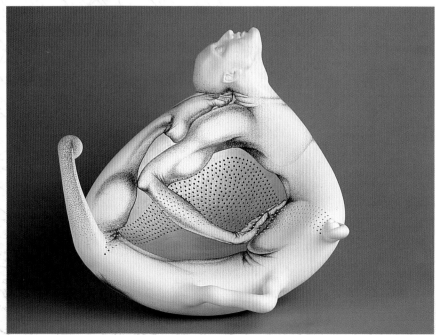

◀ **Around You** | 2002

7⅛ x 13¾ x 11 inches (18 x 35 x 28 cm)
Slip-cast porcelain; unglazed; electric
fired, cone 10; polished; china paints,
gold luster, cone 018
Photo by artist

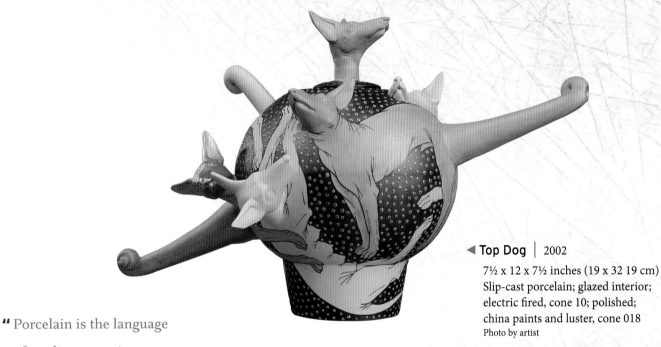

◀ **Top Dog** | 2002

7½ x 12 x 7½ inches (19 x 32 19 cm)
Slip-cast porcelain; glazed interior;
electric fired, cone 10; polished;
china paints and luster, cone 018
Photo by artist

" Porcelain is the language
of my literature; it
should be fluent and
flawless but not surpass
the idea itself. "

**Depending on
Circumstances** | 2001 ▶

7⅛ x 13¾ x 5¾ inches
(18 x 35 x 14.5 cm)
Slip-cast porcelain; glazed interior;
electric fired, cone 10; polished;
china paints, cone 018
Photo by artist

ILONA ROMULE

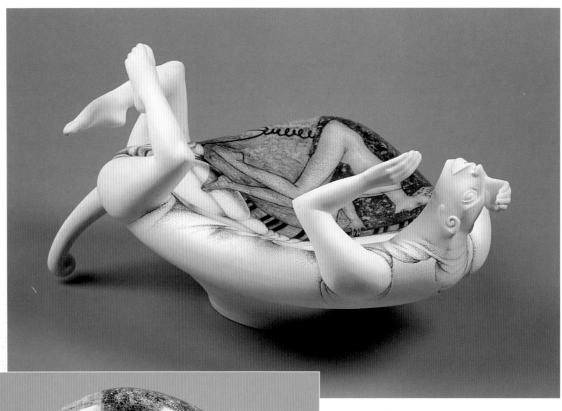

▲ **Play** | 2003

7½ x 13⅜ x 9½ inches (19 x 34 x 24 cm)
Slip-cast porcelain; partially glazed;
electric fired, cone 10; polished; china
paints and luster, cone 018
Photos by artist

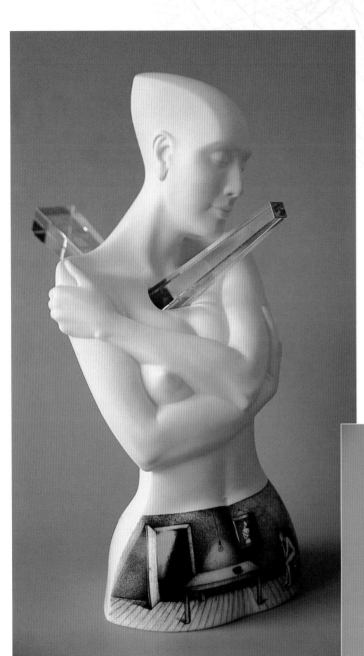

" In our partnership, I am using porcelain as a medium to communicate with the outside, but porcelain is trying to control my temper. I need to collaborate with porcelain to subdue and adapt it to my ideas. Its purity, fineness, fragility, and translucency help me reach harmony among idea, form, and surface. I love porcelain too much to change to a faster-and-easier material. "

◀ **Open Door**, 2005

14½ x 6¼ x 9¾ inches (37 x 16 x 25 cm)
Slip-cast porcelain; partially glazed; gas fired
in reduction, cone 11; polished; china paints,
cone 018; glass
Photos by artist

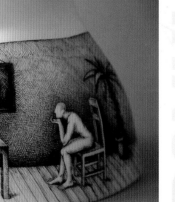

Janet DeBoos

NOTED AUSTRALIAN porcelain artist Janet DeBoos works well within the vessel tradition. She explores the possibilities of the medium, and—especially when using the potter's wheel—records the spin, twist, and flow of the clay's changes. When opting for pure whiteness, DeBoos plays off the cleanliness of industrial porcelain, but with a much more human result. Her best sets of objects succeed when exploiting this pure white, but her other works use the juxtaposition of overglaze decals with simple linear brushwork to call into question certain conventions about ceramic decoration and perhaps ceramic form itself.

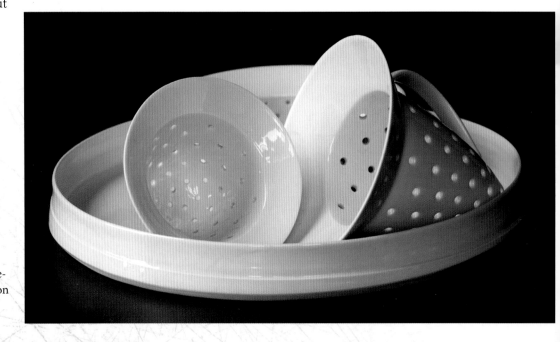

Separate (3 Sieves & Tray) | 2006

Set: 6¾ x 12½ inches (17 x 32 cm)
Wheel-thrown and pierced Australian porcelain; clear glaze; oxidation fired in gas kiln, cone 9
Photo by Karen O'Clery

▲ **Garden (Large Vase)** | 2000

12½ x 12 inches (32 x 30.5 cm)
Wheel-thrown Australian porcelain; clear glaze;
oxidation fired in gas kiln, cone 9
Photo by Rob Little, Digital Imaging
Courtesy of the National Gallery of Australia

▲ **Set Theory—Endless
Possibilities** │ 2006

Tallest cup: 6⅛ x 3⅛ inches (15.5 x 8 cm)
Wheel-thrown Australian Southern Ice
porcelain; clear glaze; oxidation fired in gas
kiln, cone 9; overglaze enamels and decals;
fired, cone 012
Photo by Stuart Hay, ANU Photography

Soft │ 2005 ▶

5⅛ x 10⅝ inches (13 x 27 cm)
Wheel-thrown Australian porcelain; clear
glaze; oxidation fired in gas kiln, cone 9
Photo by Stuart Hay, ANU Photography

" Proper lighting shows the translucence of porcelain—the light-transmitting, milky smoothness that is its preserve. "

▲ **Kanazawa Series, Solitary Pleasures–Tea** | 2005

Set: 5⅛ x 9 inches (13 x 23 cm)
Wheel-thrown Australian porcelain; clear glaze;
oxidation fired in gas kiln, cone 9; overglaze enamels
and decals, cone 012
Photo by Karen O'Clery

" One of the great wonders of porcelain is that it looks so fragile, yet is so strong. I want all my work to have that sense of *special*, even the domestic ware. Especially the domestic ware! "

▲ **Untitled** | 2005

Tallest piece: 8¼ x 2½ inches (21 x 6.5 cm)
Wheel-thrown Australian porcelain; clear glaze;
oxidation fired in gas kiln, cone 9
Photo by Stuart Hay, ANU Photography

▲ **Garden (Large Vase)** | 2001

12½ x 12 inches (32 x 30.5 cm)
Wheel-thrown Australian Southern Ice porcelain;
clear glaze; oxidation fired in gas kiln, cone 9
Photo by artist
Courtesy of the National Gallery of Australia

▲ **Saladier** | 2002

Set: 9¾ x 11¾ inches (25 x 30 cm)
Wheel-thrown Australian porcelain;
clear glaze; oxidation fired in gas
kiln, cone 9
Photo by Rob Little, Digital Imaging

Solitary Pleasures–Tea | 2002 ▲

4⅜ x 12¼ inches (11 x 31 cm)
Wheel-thrown Australian porcelain;
oxidation fired in gas kiln, cone 9
Photo by Rob Little, Digital Imaging

Studio Ware | 2001 ▶

Various sizes
Wheel-thrown Australian porcelain;
clear glaze; oxidation fired in gas
kiln, cone 9
Photo by artist

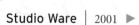

" How was it that I came to
use porcelain? It was really
very prosaic, a decision in
service to an idea. I had
made hundreds of stoneware
bowls for a show that
repeated the same gesture
over and over. But I wanted
to make three bowls of
a quite different kind to
say that these were not
only different, but special.
Porcelain. Of course. "

Watering Series | 2005 ▶

Set: 16½ x 7⅞ inches (42 x 20 cm)
Wheel-thrown Australian porcelain; clear
glaze; oxidation fired in gas kiln, cone 9
Photo by Karen O'Clery

JANET DE BOOS

Rebecca Harvey

IN HER COLORFUL, BEAUTIFULLY CONSTRUCTED WORK, Rebecca Harvey plays with stereotypical ideas of what useful ceramics can be, carefully working the boundaries of kitsch, souvenirs, classic modern tableware, and assemblage. Toasters, ducks, and platters all wear camouflage-like polka dots on colorful glazes.

Using combinations of thrown and mold-made ceramics, Harvey creates functional ware that makes us laugh, but also questions usefulness and even suggests, at times, bizarre science experiments gone wrong.

▲ **Pump−Reduction Series** | 2006
7 x 9 x 6 inches (17.8 x 23 x 15.2 cm)
Slip-cast porcelain; electric fired, cone 6
Photo by artist

▲ **Sink–Looks Like Series** │ 2003

  6 x 4 x 4 inches (15.2 x 10.2 x 10.2 cm)
  Press-molded and assembled porcelain;
  electric fired, cone 6
  Photo by artist

Two–Looks Like Series │ 2005 ▶

  8 x 6 x 5 inches (20.3 x 15.2 x 12.7 cm)
  Slip-cast porcelain; electric fired, cone 6
  Photo by artist

" I would rather go into a museum to look at a bucket than a painting, rather see 14th-century dishes than a marble statue. Patterns, shapes, and materials add up to a meaning that resonates beyond the visual. Useful objects—things made by hands for hands to use—are invitations to participate in the world; they crack open history. **"**

▲ **Anomaly—Patterns of Proliferation Series** | 1998

4 x 3½ x 8 inches (10.2 x 9 x 20.3 cm)
Slip-cast and assembled porcelain; electric fired, cone 6
Photo by artist

▲ **Toaster–Charm Series** │ 2001

   5 x 3 x 6 inches (12.7 x 7.5 x 15.2 cm)
   Press-molded and assembled porcelain;
   electric fired, cone 6
   Photo by artist

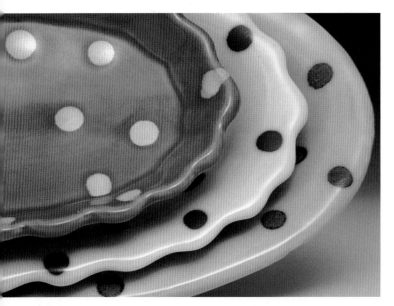

◀ **Pot Plates–Loss and Recovery Series,** │ 2001

   1 x 4 x 10 inches (2.5 x 10.2 x 25.5 cm)
   Press-molded porcelain; electric fired, cone 6
   Photo by artist

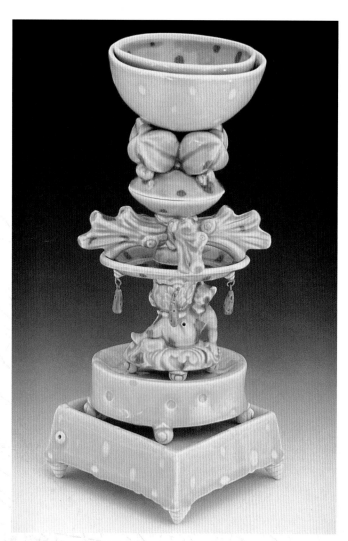

▲ **Schemes of Classification–Systema Naturae** │ 2000

12 x 13 x 5 inches (30.5 x 33 x 12.7 cm)
Press-molded and assembled porcelain; electric fired, cone 6
Photo by artist

▲ **The Hills Have Eyes–Allegorical Domestic** │ 2001

12 x 4 x 4 inches (30.5 x 10.2 x 10.2 cm)
Press-molded and assembled porcelain; electric fired, cone 6
Photo by artist

" Porcelain has such a great story—full of secrecy, lust, and covetousness. "

▲ **Ping Upside–Allegorical Domestic** | 2002

5 x 4 x 7 inches (12.7 x 10.2 x 17.8 cm)
Press-molded and assembled porcelain; electric fired, cone 6
Photo by artist

" I love glaze—shiny, drippy, and sparkly. The dullest glaze I use still has little fissures of shine running through it, like skin on custard or crust on lava. Gloss and matte glazes flow over and around each other, twisting and tugging. Glaze acts as a recorder of gravity, marking the liquid pull of the earth. There can never be too much of it. My forms are simply a backdrop for glaze to perform."

◀ Cake—Big Series | 2006

15 x 12 x 12 inches (38 x 30.5 x 30.5 cm)
Press-molded and assembled porcelain;
electric fired, cone 6
Photo by artist

REBECCA HARVEY

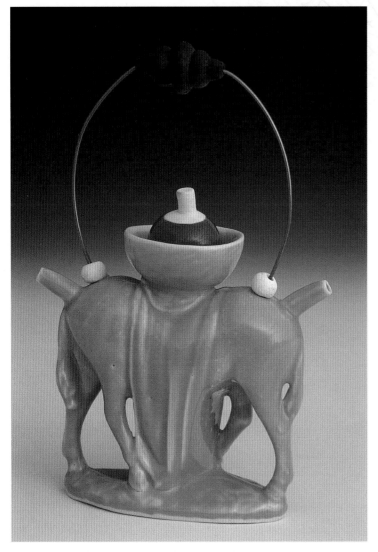

▲ **Pair−Loss and Recovery Series** │ 2001

8 x 3 x 5 inches (20.3 x 7.5 x 12.7 cm)
Press-molded porcelain; electric fired, cone 6
Photo by artist

◄ **Polo−Looks Like Series** │ 2003

8 x 4 x 9 inches (20.3 x 10.2 x 23 cm)
Slip-cast porcelain; electric fired, cone 6; wire handle
Photo by artist

Sergei Isupov

THE DREAM-LIKE, FANTASTIC porcelain figures by Sergei Isupov, with their distortions and re-combinations, create a world of their own. Isupov builds intense contrasts into these amazing forms—strangely sexual at times, seemingly innocent at others. He uses color and magnificent drawing on smooth white porcelain to create narratives that at first glance are as playful and naïve as a child's storybook, but soon reveal themselves to be as dark and mysterious as a nightmare. Isupov's juxtaposition of drawings on his superbly modeled forms plays vigorous two-dimensional scenic elements against fully sculptural figures.

◀ **Sacrifice** | 2002

12 x 6½ x 6 inches (30.5 x 16.5 x 15 cm)
Hand-built porcelain; electric fired, cone 6;
painted with colored slips and glaze
Photo by Katherine Wetzel
Courtesy of Ferrin Gallery

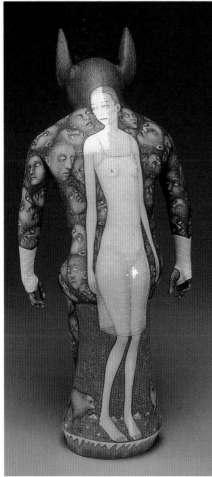

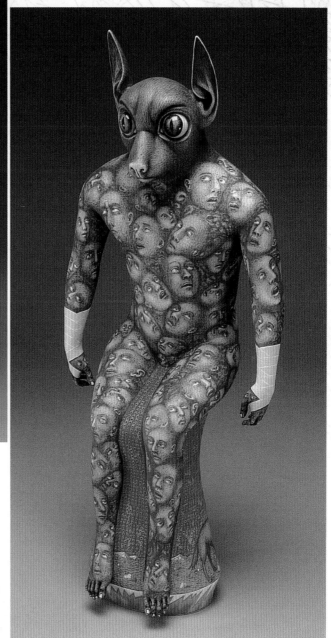

Reincarnation | 2003 ▶

20¾ x 9 x 6½ inches (52.5 x 23 x 16.5 cm)
Hand-built porcelain; electric fired, cone 6;
painted with colored slips and glaze
Photos by Katherine Wetzel
Courtesy of Ferrin Gallery

" My interest in the creative process is to build contrast. Decoration confuses form, and form fights with decoration. The piece's three dimensions make it possible to view it from different angles, offering alternate perspectives on the story.**"**

Way of Thinking, It's Like That | 1997 ▶

10½ x 15 x 6½ inches (26.5 x 38 x 16.5 cm)
Hand-built porcelain; electric fired, cone 6;
painted with colored slips and glaze
Photo by Kenneth Hayden
Courtesy of Ferrin Gallery

▲ Canceled Vacation | 1996

6½ x 11½ x 3¾ inches (16.5 x 29.2 x 9.5 cm)
Hand-built porcelain; electric fired, cone 6; painted with colored slips and glaze
Photo by John Polak
Courtesy of Ferrin Gallery

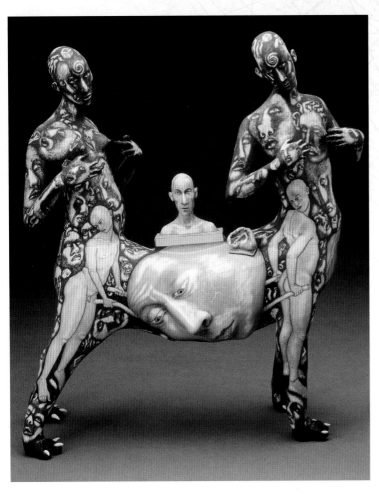

▲ **Load, Luggage** | 1997

18 x 16 x 7 inches (45.7 x 40.6 x 17.8 cm)
Hand-built porcelain; electric fired, cone 6;
painted with colored slips and glaze
Photo by Kenneth Hayden
Courtesy of Ferrin Gallery

▲ **Looking Through Darkness** | 1998

16½ x 12 x 9 inches (42 x 30.5 x 23 cm)
Hand-built porcelain; electric fired, cone 6;
painted with colored slips and glaze
Photo by Kenneth Hayden
Courtesy of Ferrin Gallery

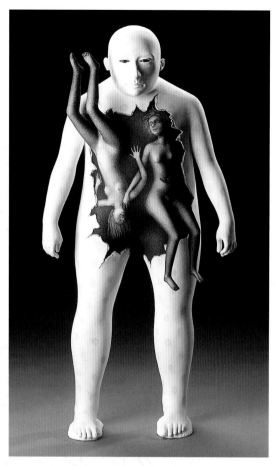

▲ **Full Moon** | 2004

22½ x 11 x 5½ inches (57 x 28 x 14 cm)
Hand-built porcelain; electric fired, cone 6;
painted with colored slips and glaze
Photo by Howard Goodman
Courtesy of Ferrin Gallery

Freeze | 1999 ▶

20 x 18 x 13 inches (50.8 x 45.7 x 33 cm)
Hand-built porcelain; electric fired, cone 6;
painted with colored slips and glaze
Photo by Kenneth Hayden
Courtesy of Ferrin Gallery

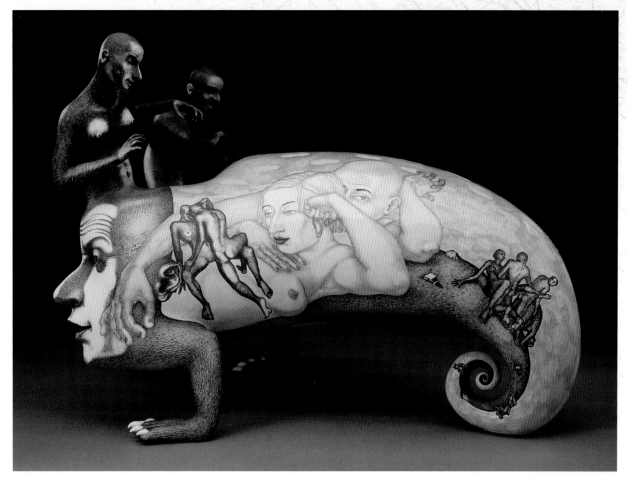

▲ **Chain** | 1999

10½ x 13½ x 9 inches (26.5 x 34.5 x 23 cm)
Hand-built porcelain; electric fired, cone 6;
painted with colored slips and glaze
Photo by Kenneth Hayden
Courtesy of Ferrin Gallery

" Art is a lifestyle for me. Everything that

surrounds and excites me is automatically

processed and transformed into the final result:

an artwork. The essence of my work is not in the

medium or in the creative process, but in human

beings and their incredible diversity "

"In the society where I grew up, working with clay was a sissy thing to do, but I couldn't find anything better for being creative. With this medium, I can be an engineer working with my hands, a designer, a painter, and a drawer—yet I am not really interested in porcelain the material; it is just a tool for me. "

Fault | 2005 ▶

17 x 14 x 5½ inches
(43 x 35.5 x 14 cm)
Hand-built porcelain; electric
fired, cone 6; painted with
colored slips and glaze
Photos by Thomas Kojcsich
Courtesy of Ferrin Gallery

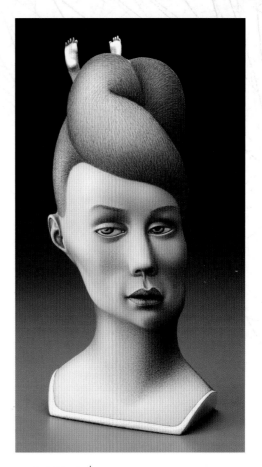

▲ **Celibacy** | 2006

 11½ x 7½ x 3 inches (29 x 19 x 7.5 cm)
 Hand-built porcelain; electric fired,
 cone 6; painted with colored slips and glaze
 Photos by John Polak
 Courtesy of Ferrin Gallery

▲ **Hot Shot** | 2006

 13 x 6 x 3½ inches (33 x 15 x 9 cm)
 Hand-built porcelain; electric fired, cone 6;
 painted with colored slips and glaze
 Photo by John Polak
 Courtesy of Ferrin Gallery

SERGEI TSUPOV

Yikyung Kim

HARKING BACK to the healthy, honest, and humble spirit of ancient Korean ceramics, the porcelain vessels of Yikyung Kim contain clean lines, white surfaces, and a sturdiness and solidity of form that is also very contemporary. The best of this work has a "rightness" that defies complete description: almost architectural at times, compositionally perfect, with a beautiful balance between line and form, foot and handle, lid and container. The quiet minimalism of Kim's work, especially in the groupings, is very modern, but their agelessness haunts the work.

▲ **Asymmetrical Placidity** │ 2002–2004

Tallest: 19¼ x 20 x 17¼ inches (49 x 51 x 44 cm)
Wheel-thrown porcelain; altered, cut, patched, and faceted;
clear glaze; gas fired in reduction, cone 10
Photo by Yi-Shik Myoung

343t ▲ Lidded Form III, 1978

9¼ x 9½ x 7⅞ inches (23.5 x 24 x 20 cm)
Wheel-thrown and altered porcelain; faceted; clear
glaze; gas fired in reduction, cone 9
Photo by Young-Woo Yoo

344t ▲ Haneul House, 1985

10¼ x 10⅝ x 8⅞ inches (26 x 27 x 22.5 cm)
Wheel-thrown speckled porcelain; altered and
faceted; clear glaze; gas fired, cone 9
Photo by Young-Woo Yoo

▲ **Vase Form** | 1985

13½ x 17⁵⁄₁₆ x 12¼ inches (34.5 x 44 x 31 cm)
Wheel-thrown, altered, cut and patched, speckled porcelain; clear glaze; reduction fired in gas kiln, cone 10
Photo by Young-Woo Yoo
Courtesy of Private Collection

▲ **Vertical Presence** | 1965

10¾ x 5 x 4¾ inches (27.5 x 12.5 x 12 cm)
Wheel-thrown and altered porcelain; faceted; clear glaze; gas fired in reduction, cone 9
Photo by Daeil Lee

" All my work begins with the thrown cylinder, which is like a canvas for the painter. While still moist, it is altered with paddles into a square form. It then goes through some cutting and patching, a process like sewing cloth. Finally, I facet it with a knife specially made by an ironsmith so it does not stick on the still-wet clay wall. "

▲ **Sewn Satchel** │ 1989

Left: 12½ x 11½ x 6 inches (32 x 29 x 15 cm); right: 12 x 10 x 6 inches (30.5 x 25.5 x 15 cm) Wheel-thrown porcelain; altered, cut, and patched; clear glaze; gas fired in reduction, cone 9
Photo by Young-Woo Yoo

YIKYUNG KIM

" Most of my work has a semi-opaque white glaze that reveals the clay body and complements the form. A subtle color effect I often use is the speckled visual texture from iron-bearing grogs in the body, which also contributes to the work's structural enhancement. These tiny flecks of darkness humanize the white field. "

▲ **Krystallos** | 1988

Tallest: 41¾ x 11¾ x 10 inches (106 x 30 x 25 cm)
Wheel-thrown porcelain; altered, cut, and patched;
clear glaze; gas fired in reduction, cone 9
Photo by Young-Woo Yoo

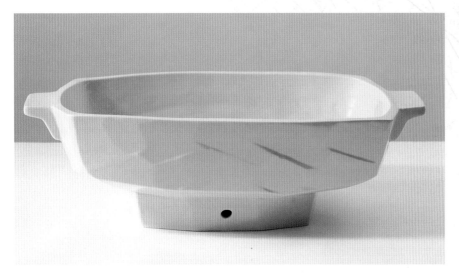

◀ **Water Vessel XII** │ 1996

6¼ x 18½ x 13 1/4 inches (16 x 47 x 33.5 cm)
Wheel-thrown and altered porcelain; faceted;
clear glaze; gas fired in reduction, cone 10
Photo by Daeil Lee

▼ **Open Form** │ 1998

9⅜ x 21⅞ x 14 inches
(24 x 55.5 x 35.5 cm)
Wheel-thrown and altered
porcelain; faceted; clear glaze;
gas fired in reduction, cone 10
Photo by Daeil Lee

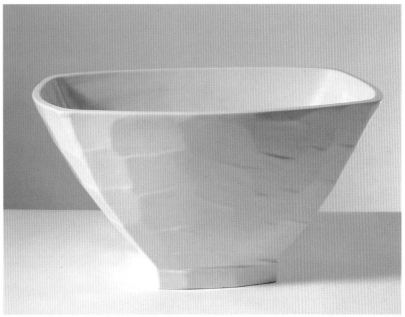

▲ **Lidded Form XV** | 1985

11⅝ x 10¾ x 9⅝ inches (29.5 x 27.5 x 24.5 cm)
Wheel-thrown speckled porcelain; altered and faceted;
clear glaze; gas fired in reduction, cone 9
Photo by Young-Woo Yoo

▲ **Lidded Jar** | 1989

22¾ x 10⅝ x 7½ inches (58 x 27 x 19 cm)
Wheel-thrown and altered porcelain; faceted;
clear glaze; gas fired in reduction, cone 10
Photo by Young-Woo Yoo

" My series of asymmetrical vessels represents the uncertainty and the dynamics of our lives. Each vessel has its own individual presence. When they are placed in a series, they give energy to each other, collectively gaining an increased harmony. The group suggests endlessness, like that of landscape. "

▲ Plateau Geometric VI │ 2004
4¾ x 17¾ x 10 inches (12 x 45 x 25.5 cm)
Slab-built and fabricated porcelain; clear glaze;
gas fired in reduction, cone 10
Photo by Yi-Shik Myoung

Les Lawrence

THE DISTINCTIVE PRINTED images on porcelain by Les Lawrence provoke both humor and thoughtfulness. With his fixation on the Mona Lisa—usually closely coupled with images of dollar bills—Lawrence creates complex collages on delicately thin porcelain slabs, and uses these to hand build teapots, cups, and vases. His use of photographic silk-screened images has inspired many ceramists. Lawrence's most recent work recalls some of his earliest, combining mold-made parts from eclectic sources with images of skulls and the like.

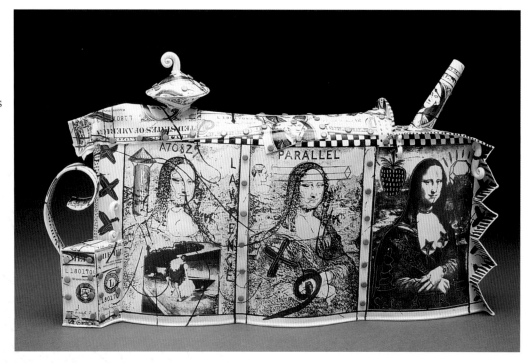

▲ **New Vision–Teapot #A70825** | 1997
7½ x 13 x 2¾ inches (19 x 33 x 7 cm)
Porcelain; photo silk-screen monoprint, slab,
stainless steel nails, wire; oxidized, cone 10
Photo by John Dixon

" Ceramics is just an excuse to start a fire. (I screened my aphorism onto T-shirts in 1991.) Many potters would fire their kilns empty just to feel the heat, smell the smoke, and see the flames. "

Shrine to Broken Cups– Neoclassical Figure | 1992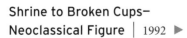

30 x 8 x 7 inches
(76.2 x 20.3 x 17.8 cm)
Porcelain sculpture clay; thrown,
slab built; engobe; oxidation,
cone 6; bronze; epoxy
Photo by artist

▲ **New Vision Vessel–Teapot #1993010** │ 1993

10 x 6 x 2½ inches (25.4 x 15.2 x 6.4 cm)
Porcelain; photo silk-screen monoprint; colored slip,
slab, stainless nails, wire; oxidation fired, cone 8
Photo by John Dixon

▲ **Galaxy–Plate** │ 1986

10 x 10 x 2 inches (25.4 x 25.4 x 5.1 cm)
Porcelain slab thrown on hump mold; colored slip,
slip trailed; cone 6, oxidation glaze
Photo by John Dixon

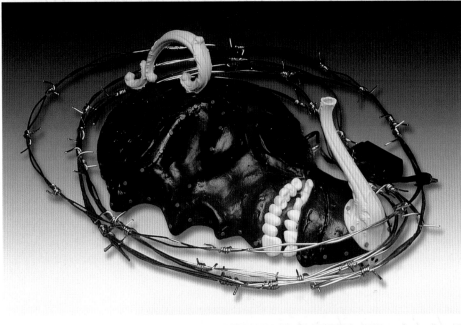

Skull Series:
Protected by Barbed Wire | 2004 ▲

6 x 14 x 4 inches (15.2 x 35.6 x 10.2 cm)
Slip-cast porcelain, black slip; photo silk-
screen monoprint, slab, stainless steel nails,
electric switch, LED battery, chrome barbed
wire, dice; oxidized, cone 10
Photo by John Dixon

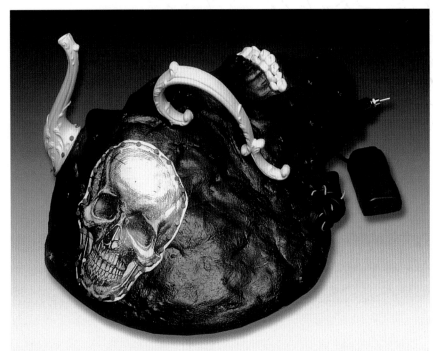

Skull Series: She Took Her Finger Off of
the Button as He Moved Away... | 2004 ▶

14 x 9 x 7 inches (35.6 x 22.9 x 17.8 cm)
Slip-cast porcelain; black slip; photo silk-
screen monoprint, slab, dice, electronic switch
circuit, LED, 9-volt battery; oxidized, cone 10
Photo by John Dixon

" I am attracted to the technology, but in the end it is about the work.

I use a photo silkscreen to print onto a glass-smooth plaster slab

with black slip. The images
are an ongoing narrative
that explores my thoughts
and observations about life.
A very thin slab of porcelain
slip then overcoats the
screened images, which is
peeled up and constructed
into vessel shapes. Porcelain
to me is the white, but I
work in the black. **"**

Garden Scape | 1991 ▶

5 x 4 x 4 inches
(12.7 x 10.2 x 10.2 cm)
Porcelain sculpture clay;
extruded; oxidation glaze;
porcelain slip, oxidation,
cone 6
Photo by John Dixon

▲ **New Vision–Cup #A70210** | 1997

13½ x 2¼ x 4 inches (34.3 x 5.7 x 10.2 cm)
Porcelain; photo silk-screen monoprint, slab,
stainless steel nails, wire; oxidized, cone 10
Photo by John Dixon

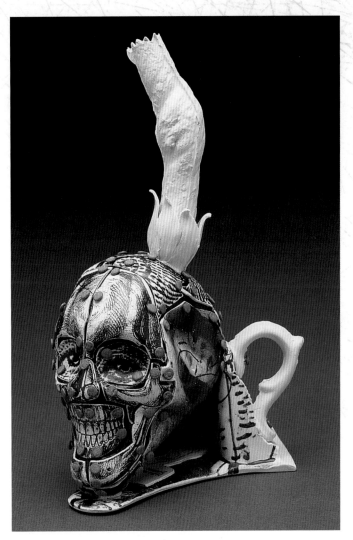

▲ **Skull Teapot #A77777** | 2002

12 x 4 x 3 inches (30.5 x 10.2 x 7.6 cm)
Slip-cast porcelain; photo silk-screen monoprint,
slab; oxidized, cone 10
Photo by John Dixon

◄ **New Vision–Teapot #A70109** │ 1997

9 x 12¼ x 2 inches (22.9 x 31.1 x 5.1 cm)
Porcelain; photo silk-screen monoprint, slab,
stainless steel nails, wire; oxidized, cone 12
Photo by John Dixon

▼ **New Vision–Teapot #A60901** │ 1995

14 x 8 x 2½ inches (35.6 x 20.3 x 6.4 cm)
Porcelain; photo silk-screen monoprint, slab,
stainless steel nails, wire; oxidized, cone 10
Photo by John Dixon

" I like everything about clay. I like the feel of the dry powdered stuff as well as the smell and feel of wet clay. My reaction to it is the same as to the smell in the desert after a few minutes of fresh rain. "

▲ New Vision—Teapot #082795 | 1995
8 x 12 x 2½ inches (20.3 x 30.5 x 6.4 cm)
Porcelain; photo silk-screen monoprint, slab, stainless
steel nails, wire; oxidized, cone 11
Photo by John Dixon

Bodil Manz

DECEPTIVELY SIMPLE in appearance, the forms by Bodil Manz are perfection in porcelain: thin, white, and translucent, perfectly decorated with geometric marks that create a sophisticated interaction between form and surface. Manz focuses on formal composition and the interplay of shadow and light. She makes fine use of the most translucent of porcelains by precisely applying graphic shapes and lines on both the interior and exterior of the vessels. Shadows from the insides lie against crisply visible exterior designs to create unusual glowing forms.

▲ **3 Pieces 2 Cylinder 1 Oval Form** │ 2003
Oval: 10¾ x 12 x 7¼ inches (27 x 30 x 18 cm);
Large cylinder: 7½ x 9¼ inches (19 x 23 cm)
Cast porcelain; transfer
Photo by Akhøj

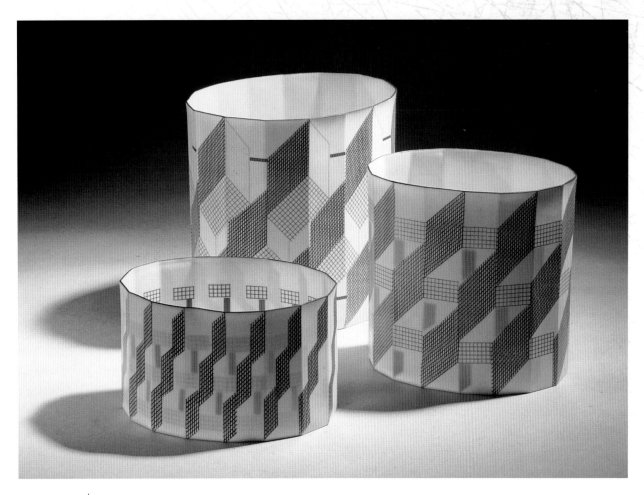

▲ **Untitled** │ 1997

    4⅛ x 5¼ x 8¾ inches (10.5 x 13.5 x 22 cm)
Cast porcelain; reduction fired, 2372°F
(1300°C), transfers, 2372°F (1300°C);
Japanese reduction, fired at 1427°F (775°C)
Photo by Akhøj

▲ **Yellow, Black, and Cromo Arancio** │ 2003

Each: 3⅛ x 3¾ inches (8 x 9.5 cm)
Cast porcelain; reduction fired at 2372°F (1300°C); decorated with high-fired
transfers, black fired at 2372°F (1300°C), Japanese yellow and cromo transfers,
1427°F (775°C)
Photo by Akhøj

▲ **Cross** | 1998

7½ x 9 inches (19 x 23 cm)
Cast porcelain; reduction fired at 2372°F (1300°C);
Decorated with high-fired transfers, Japanese
reduction fired at 1427°F (775°C)
Photo by Akhøj

Untitled | 1995 ▶

5½ x 7½ inches (16 x 19 cm)
Cast porcelain; reduction fired at 2372°F
(1300°C); black glaze, Japanese reduction fired at
1427°F (775°C) over translucent glaze
Photo by Akhøj

BODIL MANZ

" The cylinder is the simplest of forms when cast in translucent porcelain. "

◀ **Oval Form with Stepped Wall in Black & Blue** | 2006

8¾ x 11¾ x 7½ inches
(22 x 30 x 19 cm)
Cast porcelain; decorated with
high-fired transfers; gas fired in
reduction fired at 2372°F (1300°C)
Photo by Brahl

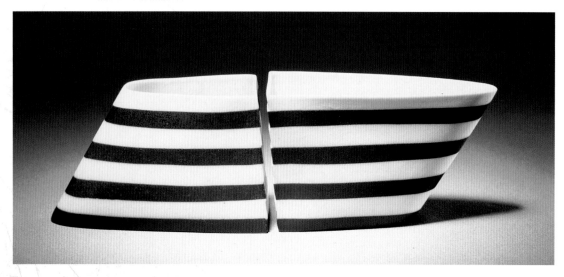

▲ **Double Parabel** | 1995

3⅛ x 3 x 5¼ inches (8 x 7.5 x 13.5 cm)
Cast porcelain; high-fired transfers; gas fired
in reduction at 2372°F (1300°C)
Photo by Akhøj

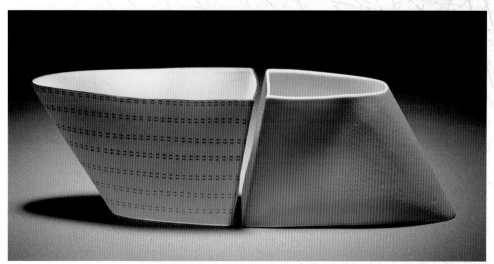

Double Parabel │ 1994 ▲

3⅛ x 3 x 5¼ inches (8 x 7.5 x 13.5 cm)
Cast porcelain; decorated with high-
fired transfers; gas fired in reduction
at 2372°F (1300°C)
Photo by Akhøj

**3 Cylinders with Yellow
and Black** │ 2001 ▶

Middle: 6¼ x 7½ inches (16 x 19 cm);
left: 4⅛ x 4½ inches (10.5 x 11.5 cm);
right: 3⅛ x 3¾ inches (8 x 9.5 cm)
Cast porcelain; reduction fired at 2372°F
(1300°C); transfers; Japanese reduction
fired at 1427°F (775°C)
Photo by Akhøj

Fragile | 2001 ▶

8¼ x 10¼ inches (27 x 26 cm)
Cast porcelain; high-fired transfers over matte white
glaze; gas fired in reduction at 2372°F (1300°C)
Photo by Brahl

▼ Pitchers in White and Black | 1992–1994

4 x 3⅛ inches (10 x 8 cm)
Cast porcelain; reduction fired, 2372°F (1300°C),
transfers, 2372°F (1300°C)

Photo by Akhøj

" Finding the innermost core of things—where they really become exciting, challenging, and difficult—is how things shift and often when the best works are created. "

▲ **2 Interrupt Oval Forms with Vine and Black Lines** │ 2000

Right: 4 x 4¾ x 3 inches (10 x 12 x 7.5 cm);
left: 3⅛ x 4 x 2⅜ inches (8 x 10 x 6 cm)
Cast porcelain, reduction fired at 2372°F (1300°C); decorated with
high-fire transfers, Japanese reduction fired at 1427°F (775°C)
Photo by Akhøj

Andrew Martin

AN EXQUISITE PORCELAIN ARTIST and amazing mold maker, Andrew Martin works with complex slip-cast forms that are usually covered with fluidly ornate brushwork. He also creates unique plaster molds for his forms, which are both modern and timeless. His influences clearly have strong roots in Middle-Eastern historical Islamic wares: strong underglaze painting, in all of its rhythmic complexity, is covered with intensely colored glazes. Art Deco notions, too, are often present. His painting on the ware shows an understanding of contemporary art and gestural painting—a unique and exciting blend.

▲ Franco-Moorish | 1997
9 x 22 x 9 ½ inches (23 x 56 x 24 cm)
Slip-cast porcelain; electric fired, cone 10
Photo by Ron Johnson

▲ **Cordoba** | 2000

9¼ x 11¼ x 4 inches (23.5 x 28.5 x 10.2 cm)

Slip-cast porcelain; electric fired, cone 10

Photo by Alleghany Meadows

" The pots must work in life; they must be attractive to pick up and compel people to return to their use, in time, again."

▲ **Abundant** | 2006

13 x 11 x 14 inches (33 x 27.9 x 35.6 cm)
Slip-cast porcelain; electric fired, cone 7
Photo by artist

▲ Rapture | 2000

9 x 13 x 4 inches
(23 x 33 x 10 cm)
Slip-cast porcelain;
electric fired, cone 10
Photo by artist

▲ Baghdad Café–A Hope
for Better Times | 2006

Set: 6 x 6 x 5½ inches (15 x 15 x 14 cm)
Slip-cast porcelain; electric fired, cone 7
Photos by artist

ANDREW MARTIN

▲ Diamond Café | 2006

2¾ x 3¾ x 4½ inches (7 x 9.5 x 11.5 cm)
Slip-cast porcelain; electric fired, cone 7
Photos by artist

Rorschach | 2006 ▼

3½ x 3½ x 5½ inches (9 x 9 x 14 cm)
Slip-cast porcelain; electric fired, cone 7
Photo by artist

▲ **Redolent Persuasion** | 1991

   18 x 11 x 3½ inches (45.5 x 28 x 9 cm)
   Slip-cast porcelain; electric fired, cone 10
   Photo by Ron Johnson

▲ **Deco Squared** | 2006

   7 x 6 x 15½ inches (18 x 15 x 39.5 cm)
   Slip-cast porcelain; electric fired, cone 7
   Photo by artist

▲ **Carthusian** | 2006

9 x 9 x 4 inches (23 x 23 x 10 cm)
Slip-cast porcelain; electric fired, cone 7
Photos by artist

" To dance with the process of beauty is the play between artists and the unseen and unknown. Receiving it, noticing it, and following where it leads is the creative process—if receiving a gift can ever be called that. **"**

▲ **Hearted Garden** | 2000

9 x 13 x 4 inches (23 x 33 x 10 cm)

Slip-cast porcelain; electric fired, cone 10

Photo by artist

Paul Mathieu

INCORPORATING LAYERS of imagery and eclectic influences, Paul Mathieu makes work that sometimes defies description. His forms contain a complex interplay of contemporary imagery, Chinese elements, classical forms, European decorative techniques, and current political and social issues. Working right at the edge of the ceramic tradition in functional wares, Mathieu subverts our stereotypes about and our ease in approaching familiar utilitarian forms by using them to address weighty issues, such as the torture at Abu Ghraib. His work calls into question many of our preconceptions about porcelain, craft, and even beauty.

▲ **Cute Boys Vase (A.R.)** | 2004

11¾ inches (30 cm) in height
Porcelain
Photo by Kumiko Yasukawa

**Tienamen Square
Flower Vases** | 2005 ▶

Each: 13¾ inches
(35 cm) in height
Porcelain
Photos by Kumiko Yasukawa

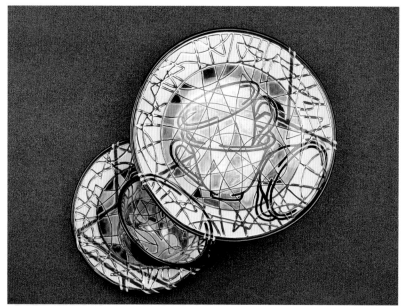

◄ **Still Life with 4 Cups** │ 1988

12 x 15 x 5 inches
(30.5 x 38.1 x 12.7 cm)
Porcelain
Photo by artist

▼ **Double Matisse Head
Flower Vase** │ 2005

27½ inches (70 cm) in height
Porcelain
Photos by Kumiko Yasukawa

" My aim is to reconcile extremes and oppositions, destroy hierarchies, and confuse conventions. Contradictions are built in, embraced, and essential."

Three Abu Ghraib Flower Vases (Brutus) | 2005 ▶

Each: 11¾ inches (30 cm) in height
Porcelain
Photo by Kumiko Yasukawa

◀ **Three Abu Ghraib Flower Vases (Venus)** | 2005

Each: 15¾ inches (40 cm) in height
Porcelain
Photo by Kumiko Yasukawa

PAUL MATHIEU

" I use porcelain because it provides a white ground for color and intense decorative surfaces. The fact that my work is made in porcelain is, by far, not the most interesting or the most important aspect of it. **"**

◀ **The Arrows of Time (for S.W.H.)** │ 1989

20 x 20 x 12 inches
(50.8 x 50.8 x 30.5 cm)
Porcelain
Photos by artist

▲ **Garniture** | 1990

　15 x 45 x 12 inches
　(38.1 x 114.3 x 30.5 cm)
　Porcelain
　Photo by artist

Amaratsu–Red Fuji | 1993 ▶

　45 x 45 x 3 inches
　(114.3 x 114.3 x 7.6 cm)
　Porcelain
　Photo by artist

▲ **Four Binary Bowls
(Smiling Buddha)** | 2004

Each: 11¾ inches
(30 cm) in diameter
Porcelain
Photos by Kumiko Yasukawa

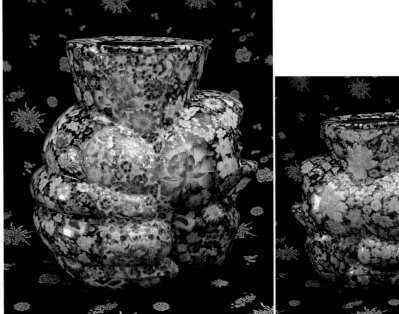

**Matisse Head Vase with
1,000 Flowers** | 2004 ▶

13¾ inches (35 cm) in height
Porcelain
Photos by Kumiko Yasukawa

" My work is not particularly well made or beautiful. In fact, it might easily be considered ugly. The materials and techniques I use are not that important or even relevant. I long for a certain anonymity, so that when, where, and by whom the object is made is at least confusing and at best irrelevant. My intent is to contest and subvert art, design, and crafts altogether. "

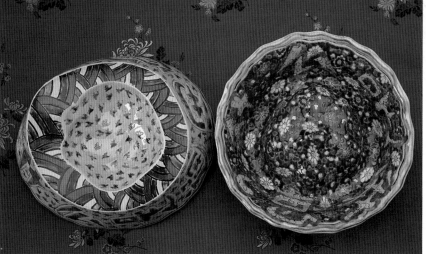

**Four Binary Bowls
(Fat Buddha)** | 2004 ▶

Each: 7⅛ inches
(18 cm) in diameter
Porcelain
Photos by Kumiko Yasukawa

Christopher P. Staley

AS EXAMPLES of thoughtful, confident work in porcelain, Christopher P. Staley's forms exude a vital energy of creation along with definite evidence of the touch of a human hand. His recent work poses pure white porcelain vessels, sometimes glazed with a delicately blue celadon glaze, against dense, black stoneware bases. His powerfully made forms set up primal interactions of light against dark, density against delicacy, strength against fragility, intent against accident, organic against geometric. Staley is a master of balancing perfect form against gesture, precisely throwing a form from porcelain clay, then softening it with a gesture of his hand. Staley clearly has a fascination for porcelain as a material and what it can do, but he uses that to talk to the viewer about what it is to be human.

▲ **Auger Platter** | 1987

27 inches (68.6 cm) in diameter
Porcelain, copper glaze
Photo by artist

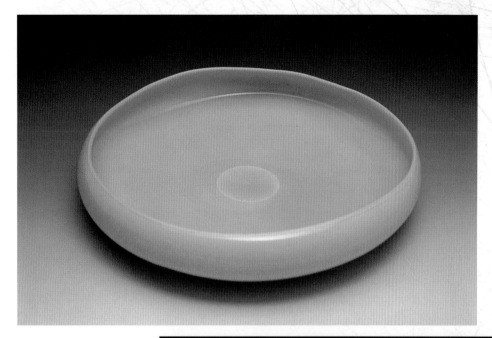

Shallow Bowl | 1996 ▲

9 x 9 x 3 inches (22.9 x 22.9 x 7.6 cm)
Wheel-thrown porcelain; celadon
glaze; fired, cone 9
Photo by artist

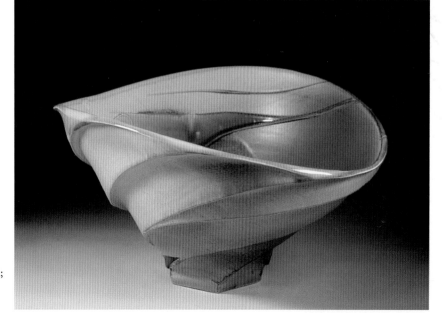

Bowl | 1988 ▶

12 x 16 x 12 inches
(30.5 x 40.6 x 30.5 cm)
Wheel-thrown porcelain; faceted;
glaze; salt fired, cone 9
Photo by artist

▲ Still-Life | 1994

14 x 8 x 7 inches (35.6 x 20.3 x 17.8 cm)
Thrown and altered porcelain; celadon glaze; fired,
cone 9; stoneware base
Photo by artist

◄ Teapot | 1985

9 x 10 x 10 inches (22.9 x 25.4 x 25.4 cm)
Wheel-thrown porcelain; slip added to surface;
glaze; salt fired, cone 9
Photo by artist

" Every touch has a meaning—from the softness of a baby's cheek to the beach sand between my toes. I believe touch has the potential to make our world larger. The smoothness and whiteness of porcelain remind me of the seductive qualities of water. Porcelain is clean and white like snow and feels refreshing, like taking a shower.**"**

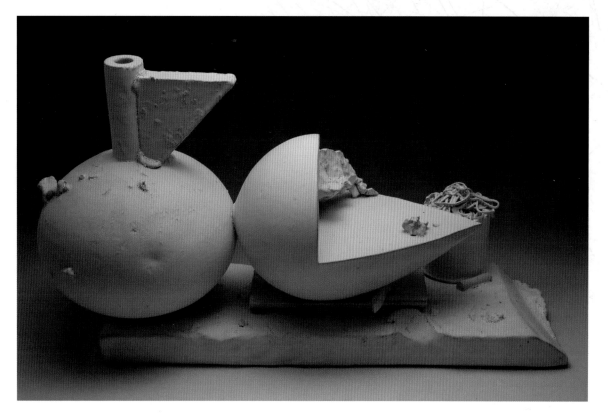

▲ **White Still-Life** │ 2006

23 x 15 x 9 inches (58.4 x 38.1 x 22.9 cm)
Porcelain; glaze; sandblasted
Photo by artist

" Clay doesn't lie. It is direct and honest in its response to touch. I believe it is the immediate consequences of our touch that make clay so satisfying to work with. It reminds me that I have a body and do not solely exist in my mind and eyes.**"**

▲ **Teapot and Two Cups** │ 1999

9 x 8 x 8 inches (22.9 x 20.3 x 20.3 cm)
Thrown and altered porcelain; celadon
glaze; fired, cone 9
Photo by artist

Still-Life | 2000 ▲

12 x 5 x 5 inches
(30.5 x 12.7 x 12.7 cm)
Hand-built porcelain; salt fired,
cone 9; stoneware base
Photo by artist

Four Cups | 2000 ▶

12 x 12 x 3 inches
(30.5 x 30.5 x 7.6 cm)
Porcelain clay dug from
ground; thrown and
altered; salt fired, cone 9
Photo by artist

▲ **Covered Jar** | 1990

15 x 8 x 8 inches (38.1 x 20.3 x 20.3 cm)
Altered porcelain, combined with black clay
Photo by artist

Auger Vase, | 1987 ▶

32 x 15 x 15 inches (81.3 x 38.1 x 38.1 cm)
Wheel-thrown porcelain; faceted; glaze;
salt fired, cone 9
Photo by artist

" In the end, clay's formlessness is its greatest gift. This trait affords infinite possibilities of becoming."

▲ **Platter** | 1989

21 inches (53.3 cm) in diameter
Slip-cast and altered porcelain; glaze;
salt fired, cone 9
Photo by artist

Richard Shaw

THE ACKNOWLEDGED MASTER of trompe l'oeil contemporary porcelain sculpture, Richard Shaw uses a huge library of molds to create simultaneously humorous and serious porcelain collages in three dimensions. Using photographic ceramic decals and delicate underglaze painting, Shaw completes the magic of making porcelain appear as objects made from a multitude of other materials. Transforming everyday objects into the fragile medium of porcelain, he forces us to reconsider them in their new context. His use of the still-life format filled with familiar things which are coupled with very human elements and modifications (the scrawled comment here, the idle doodling there), along with clever book titles and product names, connects the viewer quickly and comfortably but ultimately evokes a much more contemplative investigation of one's place in the human race.

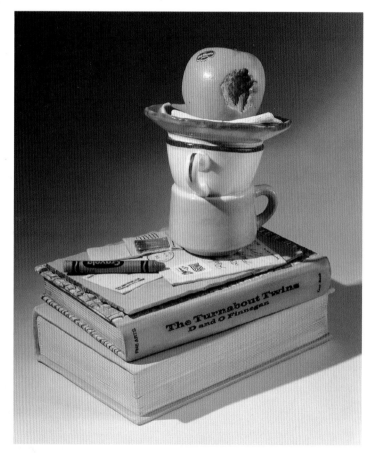

▲ **Three Stack Jar with Apple** | 1998
15½ x 10¼ x 9 inches (39.5 x 26 x 23 cm)
Slip-cast and slab-built porcelain; fired, cone 6; overglaze decals, cone 018
Photo by Schopplein Studio

▲ **Looking Around** | 2005

  15 x 9 x 6½ inches (38 x 23 x 16.5 cm)
  Wheel-thrown, slip-cast, and slab-built porcelain;
  glaze; fired, cone 6; overglaze decals, cone 018
  Photo by Charles Kennard

Seated Figure with Landscape | 2005 ▶

  32 x 14 x 13 inches (81.5 x 35.5 x 33 cm)
  Slip-cast porcelain; glaze; fired, cone 6;
  overglaze decals, cone 018
  Photo by Charles Kennard

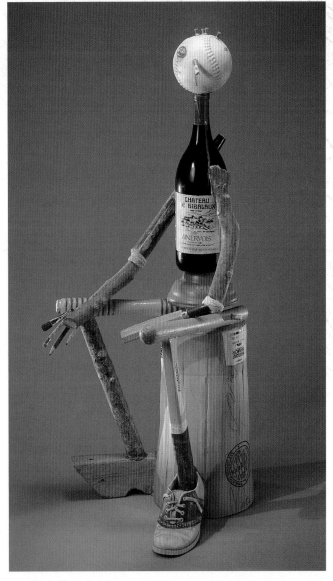

" Most of my early work was
hand-built and thrown, using
the container form as a format
for my ideas to apply my
training as a painter. I switched
from painting to ceramics
because the ceramics professors
stressed originality, personal
expression, and no rules. "

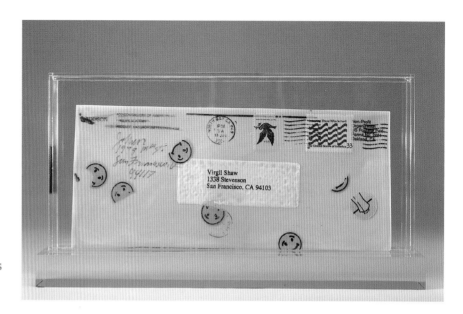

▲ **Envelope with Crows** | 2005
10 x 4¾ inches (25.5 x 12 cm)
Slip-cast porcelain; engobe pencil; underglaze inks;
glaze; fired, cone 6; overglaze decals, cone 018
Photos by Charles Kennard

He Has Faced | 1994 ▲

6½ x 10 x 13½ inches
(16.5 x 25.5 x 34.3 cm)
Slip-cast and slab-built porcelain;
combed slip; fired, cone 6; overglaze decals, cone 018
Photo by Schopplein Studio

Eraser House | 1996 ▶

12½ x 9½ x 12½ inches
(31.8 x 24 x 31.8 cm)
Slip-cast and slab-built porcelain;
glaze; fired, cone 6; overglaze
decals, cone 018
Photo by Schopplein Studio

RICHARD SHAW

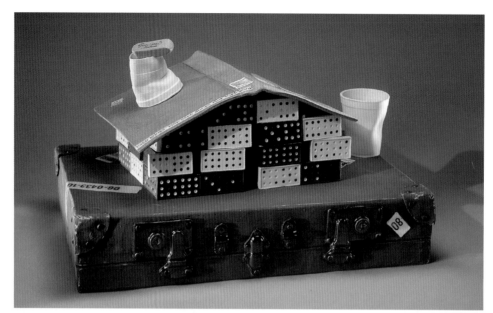

▲ **Domino House on Briefcase** | 1998

10½ x 18½ x 13 inches
(26.7 x 47 x 33 cm)
Slip-cast and slab-built
porcelain; glaze; fired,
cone 6; overglaze de-
cals, cone 018
Photo by Charles Kennard

Vanitas with Artist's Sketchbook | 2004 ▶

8 x 26 x 12 inches
(20.3 x 66 x 30.5 cm)
Slip-cast porcelain; engobe
pencil; underglaze inks;
glaze; fired, cone 6; overglaze decals, cone 018
Photo by Charles Kennard

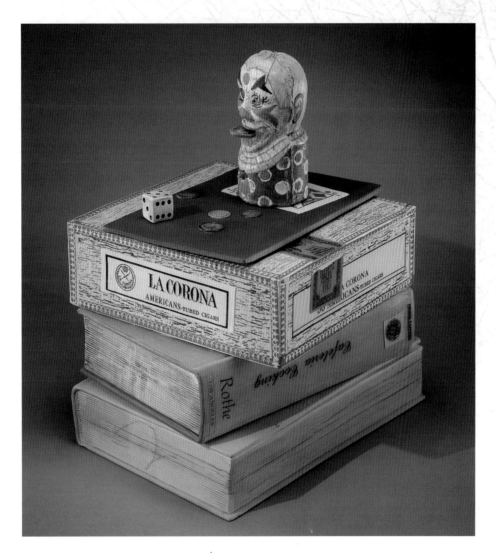

▲ **G.W.B. and Other Jokers Jar** | 2006

11½ x 10 x 8 inches (29.2 x 25.5 x 20.3 cm)
Slip-cast, slab-built porcelain; glaze; fired, cone 6;
lusters and overglaze decals, cone 018
Photo by Charles Kennard

" Working in porcelain offers several advantages: the high firing temperature creates a hard, translucent surface but the stains, oxides, and commercial underglazes I use have a natural, painterly, matte palette without having to add a coat of clear glaze over it. I worked with the silkscreen artist Wilson Burrows to develop the screen-print overglaze decal process that I use to apply and fire graphic-image printed matter to my work."

▲ Rejected Lover Teapot │ 2003
7 x 8 inches (17.8 x 20.3 cm)
Wheel-thrown and slip-cast porcelain; glaze; fired,
cone 6; overglaze decals, cone 018
Photo by Charles Kennard

RICHARD SHAW

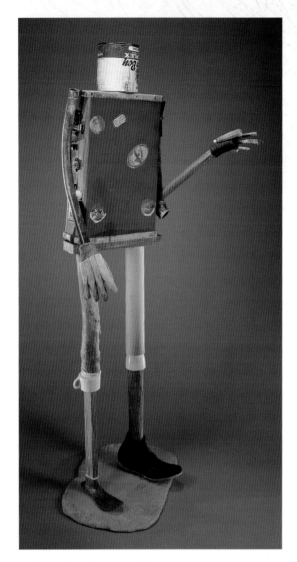

▲ **Standing Figure with Black Galosh** │ 2003

    63 x 21 x 22 inches (160 x 53.3 x 56 cm)

    Slip-cast, slab-built porcelain; glaze; fired, cone 6; newsprint transfers and overglaze decals, cone 018

    Photo by Charles Kennard

▲ **PaintBox Jar with Balboa Watercolor** │ 2003

    4 ¾ x 13 x 9½ inches (12 x 33 x 24 cm)

    Slip-cast and slab-built porcelain; underglaze painting; glaze; fired, cone 6; overglaze decals, cone 018

    Photo by Charles Kennard

Susan Beiner

THE OPULENT PORCELAIN sculptures created by Susan Beiner exude energy through a vibrant color palette and an exuberant massing of smaller forms. Drawing on the long history of European decorative ceramics, Beiner gathers together industrial forms to create complex organic images that surprise, confuse, and entertain. Using press-molded and slip-cast parts often made from molds taken from actual industrial hardware, such as lag screws, bolts, and fittings, Beiner softens these forms with slip, flowing glazes, and soda-firing, calling into question what is real and what synthetic. Her earliest work in this manner was encrusted in hardware and often entirely covered with metallic lusters, but it has steadily become a more organic mixture of shapes enhanced by soft, floral color.

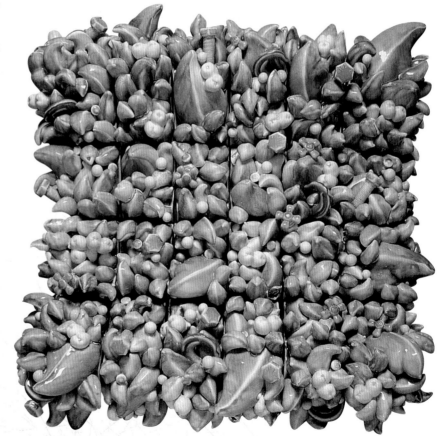

Perpetual Recollection; Desire | 2004 ▶
  45 x 52 x 8 inches (114.3 x 132 x 20.3 cm)
  Slip-cast porcelain; glaze, cone 7;
  gas fired in reduction
  Photo by Susan Einstein

▲ **Tropical Cyclone** | 2001

10 x 16 x 16 inches (25.4 x 40.6 x 40.6 cm)
Slip-cast, hand-built porcelain; glaze;
salt-fired, cone 10
Photo by Susan Einstein

" I appropriate forms from my environment and translate them into pieces of contemporary ornamentation. Their obsessive quality stems from a sense of undirected energy that became part of my personal expression. **"**

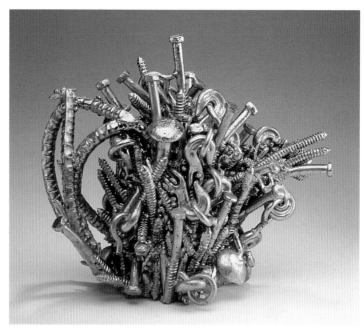

▲ **Bolted and Screwed** | 1998

12 x 10 x 8 inches (30.5 x 25.4 x 20.3 cm)
Slip-cast porcelain; glaze, cone 6; gas fired;
luster, cone 018
Photo by Tim Thayer

◀ **Nesting** | 2000

17 x 13 x 14½ inches (43.2 x 33 x 36.8 cm)
Slip-cast porcelain; glaze, cone 6; gas fired;
luster, cone 018
Photo by Susan Einstein

▲ **Screwed Mantle Jars** | 1998

    26 x 7 x 7 inches (66 x 17.8 x 17.8 cm)
    Slip-cast porcelain; glaze, cone 6; gas fired;
    luster, cone 018
    Photo by Tim Thayer

▲ **Journey** | 1996

    8 x 6 x 5 inches (20.3 x 15.2 x 12.7 cm)
    Slip-cast porcelain; gas fired glaze, cone 6;
    electric fired glaze, cone 06; luster, cone 018
    Photo by artist

SUSAN BEINER

" Recently, I've become interested in contrasting the purity of porcelain with the artificial qualities of industrially processed materials, such as plastics, rubber, and foam. What will be next is yet to be discovered."

▲ **Rather than Obliquely Encoded** | 2005
32 x 38 x 44 inches (81.3 x 96.5 x 111.8 cm)
Hand-built, slip-cast porcelain; glaze, cone 7; gas fired;
thermoplastic; small rubber parts attached
Photos by Robert Wedemeyer

▲ **English Garden** | 1997

  28 x 13 x 9 inches (71.1 x 33 x 22.9 cm)
  Slip-cast porcelain; glaze, cone 10;
  gas fired; luster, cone 018
  Photo by Tim Thayer

◀ **Candelabra** | 1997

  54 x 18 x 18 inches
  (137.2 x 45.7 x 45.7 cm)
  Slip-cast porcelain, made in four sections; gas
  fired, cone 6; luster, cone 018
  Photo by artist

" I admire the shapes of hardware, though I strive to negate their intended function by utilizing them as organic specimens rather than as industrial fasteners. "

▲ **Encrusted Soup Tureen with Candlesticks,** | 1999
Tureen: 10 x 18 x 12 inches (25.4 x 45.7 x 30.5 cm);
candlesticks: 11 x 4 x 5 inches (27.9 x 10.2 x 12.7 cm)
Slip-cast, hand-built porcelain; glazed, cone 10; salt fired
Photo by Susan Einstein

▲ **In Parallel I** │ 2006

   12 x 11 x 7 inches
   (30.5 x 27.9 x 17.8 cm)
   Slip-cast porcelain; glaze,
   cone 7; gas fired
   Photo by John Carlano

▲ **New Hybrid** │ 2004

   7 x 7 x 7 inches (17.8 x 17.8 x 17.8 cm)
   Slip-cast porcelain; glaze, cone 7; gas fired
   Photo by Susan Einstein

SUSAN BEINER

Curtis Benzle

A MASTER OF COLORED TRANSLUCENT PORCELAIN, Curtis Benzle produces incredibly thin forms that glow like stained glass. His hand-built vessels, often bowl-shaped, offer a complexity of overlapping images formed from slabs taken from intricately patterned blocks of colored porcelain. Layering these slabs, Benzle creates vessels with distinctly different interior and exterior patterns that merge softly as light floods through the thin porcelain. His work draws the viewer into an intimate reality with a vision that initially suggests a landscape but ultimately is more personal and colorful.

Life Flutters By │ 2003 ▶

7 x 7 x 4 inches (17.8 x 17.8 x 10.2 cm)
Hand-built porcelain; nerikomi, slip painting, inlay; unglazed; electric fired, cone 8; 23k gold leaf
Photo by artist

" I struggle with difficult materials, invent frustrating techniques, and tolerate relentless failure. My goal is both elusive and seductively possible. I have an unfailing desire to give form to feeling—to connect myself and my audience with a better place and to express some of what is so wonderful in our world."

▲ **Renewal** | 2003

8 x 18 x 3 inches (20.3 x 45.7 x 7.6 cm)
Hand-built porcelain; nerikomi, slip painting, inlay;
unglazed; electric fired, cone 8; 23k gold leaf
Photos by artist

▲ **Sanctuary Lighting** | 2004

10 x 192 x 6 inches (25.5 x 488 x 15.2 cm)
Hand-built porcelain; slip painting;
unglazed; electric fired, cone 8;
Plexiglas core and fluorescent light
Photos by artist

" Porcelain, pattern, color, and light are some of the keys available to aid me in unlocking beauty. While finding the right sequence and order can be challenging, every slight success excites my passion to continue this quest. "

◀ **East Wind** | 2003

12 x 23 x 4 inches (30.5 x 58.5 x 10.2 cm)
Hand-built porcelain; nerikomi, slip painting, inlay; unglazed; electric fired, cone 8; 23k gold leaf
Photo by artist

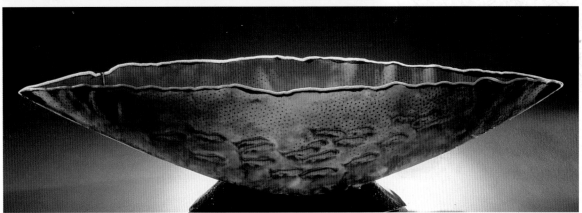

▲ **Following Sea** | 2004

6 x 19 x 4 inches (15.2 x 48.3 x 10.2 cm)
Hand-built porcelain; nerikomi, slip painting, inlay; unglazed; electric fired, cone 8; 23k gold leaf
Photo by artist

CURTIS BENZLE

◄ **Memories of Hope** │ 2002

8 x 18 x 3 inches (20.3 x 45.7 x 7.5 cm)
Hand-built porcelain; nerikomi, slip
painting, inlay; unglazed; electric fired,
cone 8; 23k gold leaf
Photo by artist

Flying Home │ 2002 ▶

9 x 18 x 3 inches (23 x 45.7 x 7.5 cm)
Hand-built porcelain; nerikomi, slip
painting, inlay; unglazed; electric
fired, cone 8; 23k gold leaf
Photo by artist

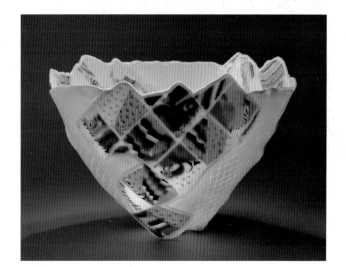

▲ **Autumn Dreams** | 2003

48 x 14 x 10 inches (122 x 35.5 x 25.5 cm)
Hand-built porcelain; slip painting;
unglazed; electric fired, cone 8;
Plexiglas core and fluorescent light
Photos by artist

▲ **Broadway Boogie** | 1980

6 x 7 inches (15.2 x 17.8 cm)
Hand-built porcelain; nerikomi, inlay; unglazed;
electric fired, cone 8
Photo by artist

CURTIS **BENZLE**

▲ **Phoenix Rising** │ 2003

5 x 5 x 5 inches (12.7 x 12.7 x 12.7 cm)
Hand-built porcelain; nerikomi, slip painting, inlay;
unglazed; electric fired, cone 8; 23k gold leaf
Photo by artist

▲ **Leaf Pyre** │ 2004

12 x 8 x 7 inches (30.5 x 20.3 x 17.8 cm)
Hand-built porcelain; slip painting;
unglazed; electric fired, cone 8; glass core
and fluorescent light
Photo by artist

" My art has not seemed to change much over the years. The characteristics that defined it 20 years ago—color and light—remain as obvious visual evidence of my personal mission to understand and uncover expressions of beauty.**"**

▲ **Floral Group** | 2005

5 x 5 inches (12.7 x 12.7 cm)
Hand-built porcelain; nerikomi, slip painting, inlay;
unglazed; electric fired, cone 8; 23k gold leaf
Photo by artist

Philip Cornelius

WITH HIS LONG HISTORY as a worker in porcelain, Philip Cornelius creates delicately thin forms whose aggressiveness of surface and form often seems contradictory. Using slabs of porcelain (usually paper thin), Cornelius constructs small sculptural objects, such as teapots,

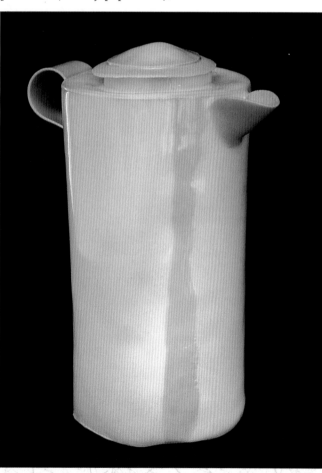

that have a surprising combination of playfulness and sadness. He is perhaps best known for his mastery of the use of high-temperature saggar firing to lay a veil of quiet grays and blacks against the hard whiteness of porcelain. In more recent works, a dry, rough, stain-colored surface unifies the diverse forms used to construct the pieces. His use of abstract form, coupled with one or two more recognizable forms, sets up a dialog that often involves a clash between the natural and the mechanical.

◀ **Pitcher with Lid** | 1974

12 x 7 x 6 inches (30.5 x 18 x 15 cm)
Thin-ware porcelain; clear glaze; gas
fired, cone 10
Photo by artist

▲ **Continental** | 1983

    12 x 14 x 4 inches (30.5 x 35.6 x 10.2 cm)

    Thin-ware porcelain; unglazed; charcoal fired, cone 10

    Photo by artist

▲ **Jack Rabbit** | 1984

    13 x 8 x 8 inches (33 x 20.3 x 20.3 cm)
Thin-ware porcelain; unglazed; gas fired,
cone 10
Photo by artist

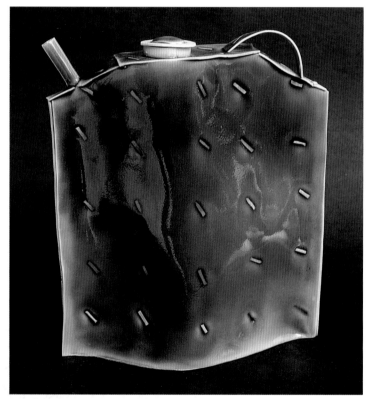

▲ **Smokin' Jack Rutile** | 1981

    7 x 7 x 3 inches (17.8 x 17.8 x 7.6 cm)
Thin-ware porcelain; Oribe glaze; gas
fired, cone 10
Photo by artist

" Working with clay is like having a conversation; I never know from one piece to the next where it will lead. Each time I go into the studio, ideas come to me through the act of physical work, which creates a kind of mystical dream state."

▲ **Slow Joe** | 1981

11 x 8 x 3 inches (27.9 x 20.3 x 7.6 cm)
Thin-ware porcelain; charcoal fired,
cone 10
Photo by artist

" Years ago, while making large plates, I developed an original "thin-ware" process of making forms from the clay left behind on the large plaster bats. I wanted to make work that was so light it would have the feeling of surprise and disbelief, and since then I produced several hundred pieces with this method.**"**

▲ **Orange Grove on a Blue Night** │ 1992

8 x 16 x 4 inches (20.5 x 40.5 x 10 cm)
Thin-ware porcelain; cobalt engobe; gas fired, cone 10
Photo by artist

River Warrior | 1991 ▲

    7 x 15 x 3 inches (18 x 38 x 7.5 cm)
Thin-ware porcelain; rutile engobe;
gas fired, cone 10
Photo by artist

Nissan Maru | 1984 ▶

    8 x 15 x 4 inches (20.3 x 38 x 10 cm)
Thin-ware porcelain; stained; charcoal
fired, cone 10
Photo by artist

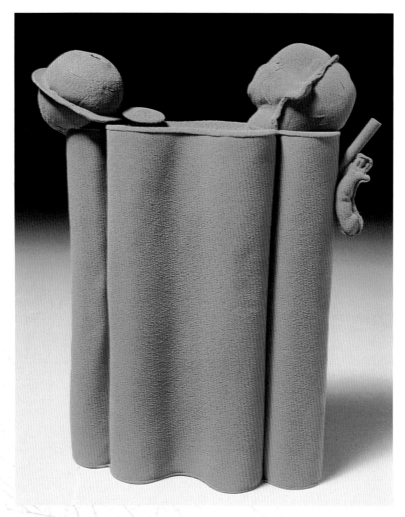

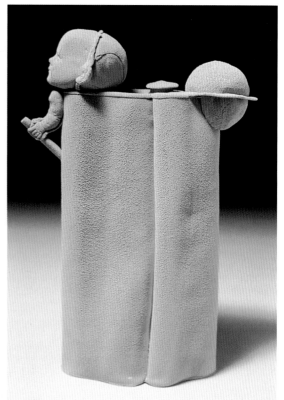

▲ **Playing** │ 1992

   14 x 8 x 4 inches (35.6 x 20.3 x 10.2 cm)
   Thin-ware porcelain; rutile engobe; gas
   fired, cone 10
   Photo by artist

▲ **Claremont** │ 1992

   6 x 3½ x 2 inches (15.2 x 8.9 x 5.1 cm)
   Thin-ware porcelain; chrome engobe;
   gas fired, cone 10
   Photo by artist

" To build the teapot form, you have to coordinate a lid, a handle, a spout, and a main, containing form, as well as, perhaps, an infuser. All these parts can be stretched, changed, and looked at in new ways. **"**

▲ **Monument** | 1992

13 x 9 x 6 inches (33 x 23 x 15 cm)
Thin-ware porcelain; chrome engobe; gas fired, cone 10
Photo by artist

Claire Curneen

THE PORCELAIN FIGURES of Claire Curneen are some of the most expressive in contemporary figurative ceramics. Their stark whiteness evokes a haunting ghostliness. Using little glaze, Curneen builds these figures by hand, letting a lot of the process show in the delicate porcelain surfaces.

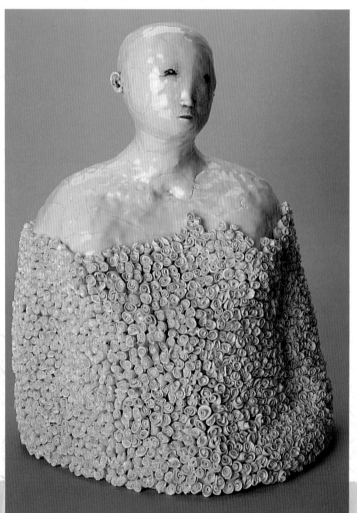

Her sculpture, often based on the religious iconography of Catholicism, communicates the saintly qualities of their subjects with expressions at once sorrowful and surprised, while carefully modeled hands make meaningful gestures.

◀ **Feast** │ 2003
21¾ x 11 x 6 inches (55 x 28 x 15 cm)
Hand-built porcelain; glaze; electric
fired, cone 2300°F (1260°C)
Photo by Dewi Tarratt Lloyd

▲ **Falling Slowly** | 2003

16½ x 11¾ x 11¾ inches (42 x 30 x 30 cm)

Porcelain; transparent glaze; electric fired, 2300°F (1260°C); decals and luster, cone 1562°F–1382°F (850°C –750°C)

Photo by artist

▲ **Figure with Branches** │ 2005

17¾ x 9 x 6¼ inches (45 x 23 x 16 cm)
Porcelain; celadon glaze; gas fired in reduction,
cone 2336°F (1280°C)
Photos by artist

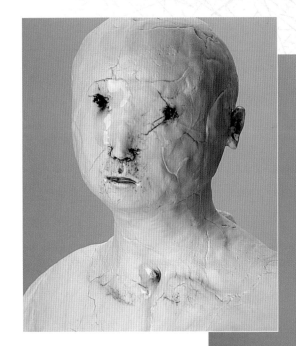

Angel | 2003 ▶

    27½ x 13¾ x 11¾ inches (70 x 35 x 30 cm)
Hand-built porcelain; partially glazed;
electric fired, cone 2300°F (1260°C); luster,
cone 1382°F (750°C)
Photos by Dewi Tarratt Lloyd

CLAIRE **CURNEEN**

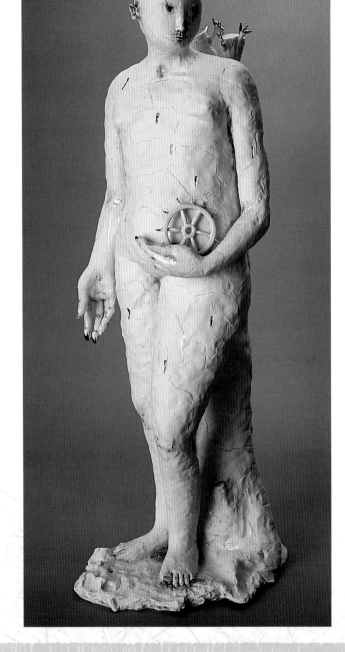

" I could never understand why, when potters talked about porcelain, they became dewy-eyed and lovesick, because I've always believed in content more than material. But one cannot help but be seduced by the alchemy of porcelain, so I look forward to more lovesickness."

◀ St. Catherine | 2003

26¾ x 11¾ x 6¼ inches (68 x 30 x 16 cm)
Hand-built porcelain; partially glazed; electric fired,
cone 2300°F (1260°C); luster, cone 1382°F (750°C)
Photo by Dewi Tarratt Lloyd

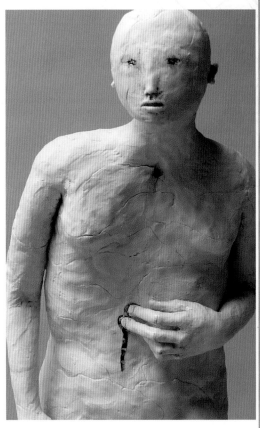

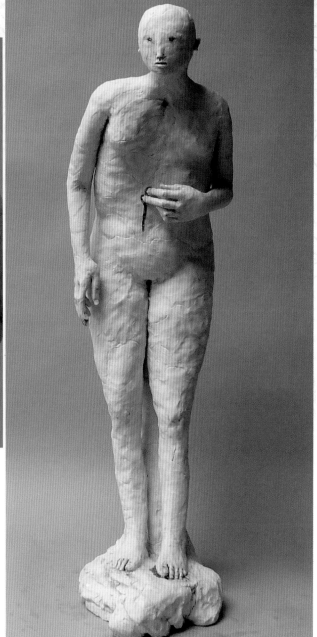

Attitude of Sorrow I │ 2004 ▶

28¾ x 9½ x 6 inches (73 x 24 x 15 cm)
Porcelain; glazed in areas; electric fired,
cone 2300°F (1260°C); luster fired, cone
1382°F (750°C)
Photos by artist

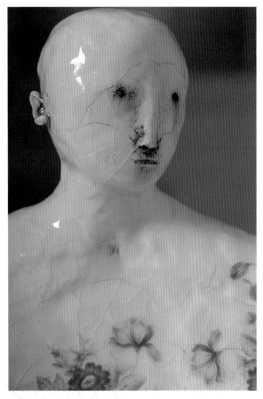

▲ **Blue Series** | 2002

15 x 11¾ x 7 inches (38 x 30 x 18 cm)
Hand-built porcelain, pinched hollow form;
transparent glaze; electric fired, cone 2300°F
(1260°C); blue flower decals, cone
1832°F (1000°C)
Photo by S. Braun

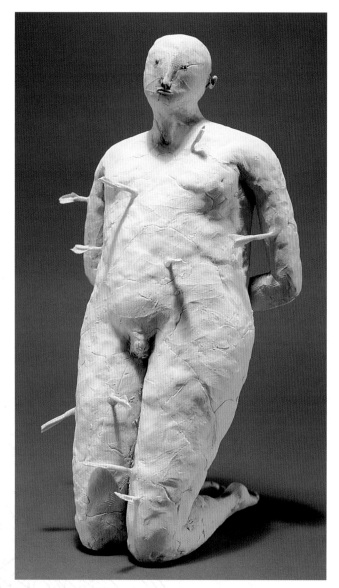

St. Sebastian | 2000 ▶

19¾ x 9¾ x 11 inches (50 x 25 x 28 cm)
Hand-built porcelain, pinched hollow form;
transparent glaze; electric fired, cone
2300°F (1260°C)
Photo by artist

" Words that we use to describe porcelain seem to be metaphors for figurative work itself: translucent, jewel-like, naked, body, memory, precious, skin."

Bird Figure | 1996 ▶

26¾ x 11 x 7 inches (68 x 28 x 18 cm)
Crank clay with porcelain slip; transparent
glaze, washes of black stain; electric fired,
cone 2300°F (1260°C)
Photos by artist

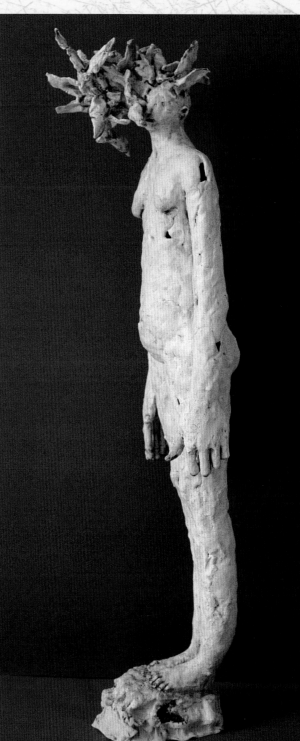

Paul A. Dresang

THE INTRICATELY FINISHED PORCELAIN SCULPTURES made by Paul A. Dresang reflect a wide range of influences, from ancient Persian pouring vessels to 20th-century oil cans and leather luggage. His complex textures, rendered delicately into the soft porcelain, are enhanced by salt-glaze firing, and by careful masking and selective sandblasting of the fired surface to reveal new colors, sometimes going back to the original whiteness of the porcelain that underlies orange-brown slips and salted surfaces. More recently, his teapots appear to be emerging from snugly fitted black leather bags, with all the seams, zippers, buckles, snaps, and rivets rendered in exquisite, realistic porcelain detail.

▲ **Doctor's Bag** | 2002
11 x 12 x 7½ inches
(28 x 30.5 x 19 cm)
Hand-built, thrown, and altered porcelain; residual salt glaze; masked and sandblasted; fired, cone 10; cone 04 and 018 luster firings
Photo by artist

▲ **Back Pack** | 2001

10 x 20 x 20 inches (25.5 x 51 x 51 cm)
Hand-built, thrown, and altered porcelain; residual
salt glaze; masked and sandblasted; fired, cone 10;
cone 04 and 018 luster firings; thermofax-screened
enamel, cone 018
Photos by artist

" Porcelain's fine texture and whiteness provides a visual clarity while I'm working, and it is capable of recording a complete range of sensual expression. Yet it also can be nurtured into the most amazingly rigid, mechanical forms that are the complete antithesis of the sensual.**"**

▲ **Untitled** │ 1988

10 x 12 x 6 inches (25.5 x 30.5 x 15 cm)
Wheel-thrown and hand-built porcelain;
residual salt glaze; masked and sandblasted;
fired, cone 10
Photo by artist

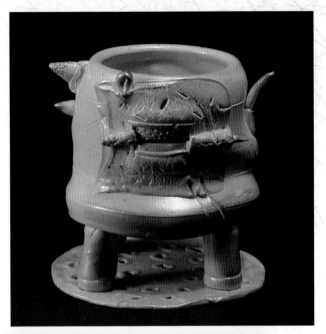

▲ **Untitled** | 1983

5 x 3½ x 3½ inches (12.5 x 9 x 9 cm)
Wheel-thrown and hand-built
porcelain; residual salt glaze; masked
and sandblasted; fired, cone 10
Photo by artist

◀ **Untitled** | 1985

8 x 9 x 5 inches (20.5 x 23 x 12.5 cm)
Wheel-thrown and hand-built porcelain; residual salt glaze; masked and
sandblasted; fired, cone 10
Photo by artist

PAUL A. **DRESANG**

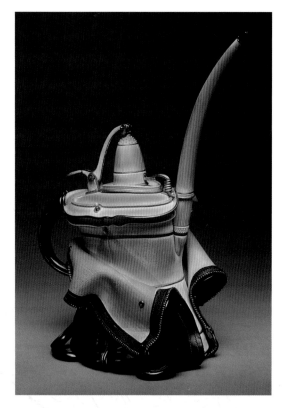

" At about age eight, I met this old country guy who showed me the collections of knots, leaves, and boats he had carved out of wood. I carved a wolf with no tail from a bar of soap and decided I liked carving. When I wasn't whittling my fingers or inadvertently stabbing myself, I made piles of shavings and little stand-up animals. I favored rearing horses. **"**

▲ **Untitled** | 1995
17 x 14 x 8 inches (43 x 35.5 x 20.5 cm)
Wheel-thrown and hand-built porcelain;
residual salt glaze; masked and sandblasted;
fired, cone 10; cone 04 and 018 luster firings
Photo by artist

Untitled | 1991 ▶
16 x 14 x 9 inches (40.5 x 35.5 x 23 cm)
Wheel-thrown and hand-built
porcelain; residual salt glaze; masked
and sandblasted; fired, cone 10
Photo by artist

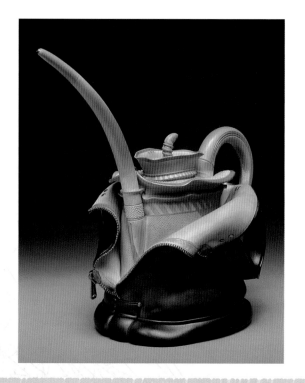

▲ Untitled | 1998

14 x 11 x 11 inches (35.5 x 28 x 28 cm)
Hand-built, thrown, and altered porcelain; residual
salt glaze; masked and sandblasted; fired, cone 10;
cone 04 and 018 luster firings
Photo by Joseph Gruber

Untitled | 1998–1999 ▶

17 x 12 x 12 inches (43 x 30.5 x 30.5 cm)
Hand-built, thrown, and altered porcelain;
residual salt glaze; masked and sandblasted;
fired, cone 10; cone 04 and 018 luster firings
Photo by artist

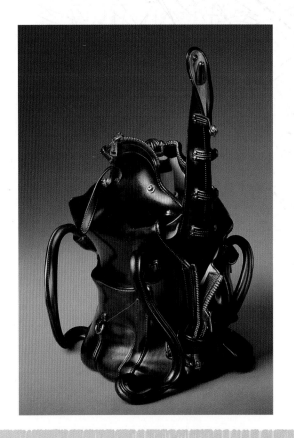

▲ **Rocket Boy** | 2000

> 10 x 19 x 12 inches (25.5 x 48.5 x 30.5 cm)
> Hand-built, thrown, and altered porcelain;
> residual salt glaze; masked and
> sandblasted; ; underglazes, cone 04; fired,
> cone 10; cone 04 and 018 luster firings;
> photo emulsion
> Photo by artist

Untitled | 1998 ▶

> 12 x 20 x 11 inches (30.5 x 51 x 28 cm)
> Hand-built, thrown, and altered por-
> celain; residual salt glaze; masked and
> sandblasted; fired, cone 10; cone 04 and
> 018 luster firings
> Photo by Joseph Gruber

" A very early raku bag series, which then presented and wholly contained the teapot, reemerged in porcelain form and, combined with other objects, eventually eclipsed those 'spouted monarchs.' At times the bag or vessel now appears solo to offer its own ambiguous tale. But in either context, such work is meant to elicit a narrative from viewers. I seduce them through the work's intricate, formal trompe l'oeil details. I hope they will want to touch it, need to touch it. "

▲ Briefcase | 2003
3½ x 18 x 16 inches (9 x 45.5 x 40.5 cm)
Slab-built porcelain; residual-salt fired;
enamels and lusters, cone 018
Photo by Matt Wilt

HOUSE

Harlan House

THE BEAUTIFUL PORCELAIN POTS by Canadian potter Harlan House are inspired by ancient Chinese pottery. His work plays between straightforward utilitarian and more sculptural concerns, staying well within the vessel-making tradition of the studio potter. Carved flowers and self-portraits on Chinese-style vases add a delicacy to the tightly thrown, almost inflated forms, as in the Green Apple Meiping. Adding a clay "shadow" to other vases injects a bit of whimsy into these historically inspired forms. In other pieces, often wood-fired, House explores the crustier side of porcelain—still playing off the Chinese forms and using applied slips and glazes along with natural wood ash glazes from the firing— to almost negate the perfection of form under these added surfaces.

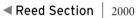

◀ **Reed Section** │ 2000
15 x 10⅝ inches (38 x 27 cm)
Wheel-thrown porcelain; carved reed decoration with self-portrait under celadon glaze; propane fired in reduction, cone 11
Photo by artist

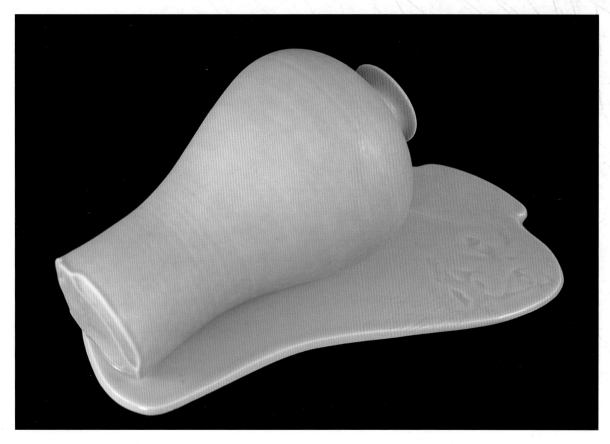

▲ **Meet Your Maker** | 2005

6¼ x 15 inches (16 x 38 cm)

Wheel-thrown HH porcelain meiping, fused to carved self-portrait shadow in Chinese porcelain; Imperial Snapdragon Yellow (meiping) and HH celadon (shadow) glazes; shells; propane fired in reduction, cone 12

Photo by artist

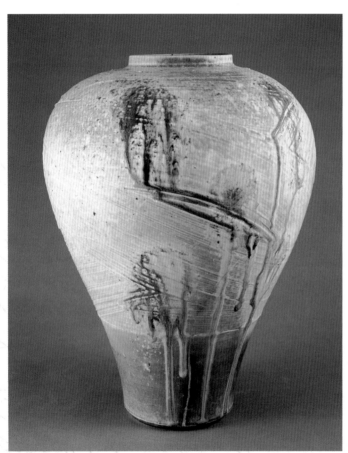

▲ **Meiping Branch Vase** | 1985

13¾ x 10⅝ inches (35 x 27 cm)
Wheel-thrown porcelain; brushed slip
decoration; copper-lithium glaze; wood
fired (on bagwall), cone 12; 24k gold leaf
Photo by artist

▲ **Tulip Branch Vase** | 1995

16⅛ x 10⅝ inches (41 x 27 cm)
Wheel-thrown porcelain; March crackle glaze, drawing
ink and wax resist; Xue Bai chicken-skin glaze; propane
fired in reduction, cone 12
Photo by artist

" My source of inspiration is in our home and garden. What happens in those places is transposed onto porcelain. When our tulips bloom, I am amazed. I set up still lifes and work directly as a painter would. Art and life are inseparable. **"**

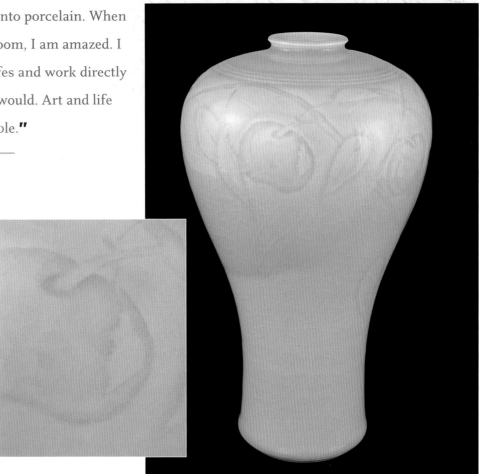

▲ **Green Apple Meiping** │ 2003

12¾ x 6¾ inches (32.4 x 17 cm)
Wheel-thrown porcelain; carved decoration
under celadon glaze; propane fired in reduction, cone 12
Photos by artist

HARLAN HOUSE

Champagne Meiping | 2001

14¼ x 7⅞ inches (36 x 20 cm)
Wheel-thrown porcelain; stenciled and combed slip
decorations; celadon glazes on stencils, Marine Wudi
glaze (on body); propane fired in reduction, cone 11
Photo by artist

My Fave | 2006 ▶

Vase: 12 x 7¼ inches (30.5 x 18.5 cm);
shadow: 15¾ x 7 inches (40 x 18 cm)
Wheel-thrown, carved porcelain
meiping; slip-cast slab shadow, cut and
carved; HH celadon (meiping) and
Dynasty Ash (shadow) glazes; propane
fired in reduction, cone 12
Photo by artist

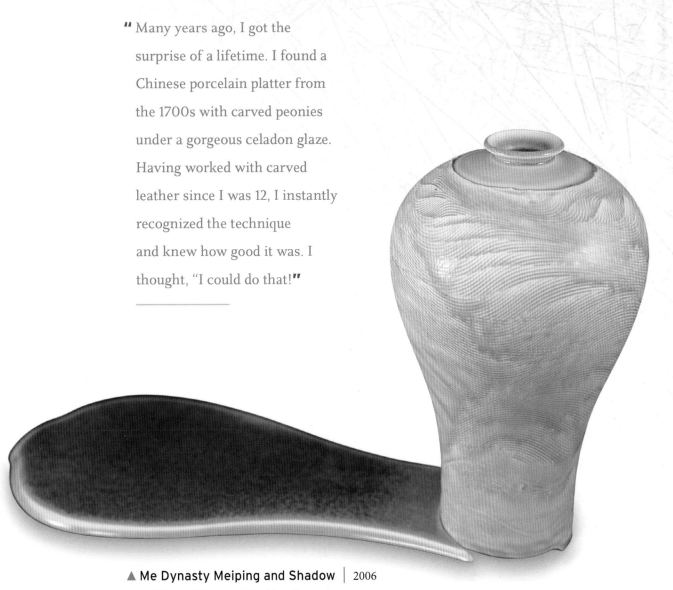

" Many years ago, I got the surprise of a lifetime. I found a Chinese porcelain platter from the 1700s with carved peonies under a gorgeous celadon glaze. Having worked with carved leather since I was 12, I instantly recognized the technique and knew how good it was. I thought, "I could do that!"

▲ **Me Dynasty Meiping and Shadow** | 2006

10⅝ x 16½ inches (27 x 42 cm)
Wheel-thrown HH porcelain meiping; hand-built Chinese porcelain shadow; combed slip decoration; Imperial Snapdragon Yellow and Dynasty Ash glazes; propane fired in reduction, cone 12
Photo by artist

" My latest works include objects and their shadows, all completed in porcelain. The shadow evokes a sense of place or belonging. As the shadow takes on a life of its own, the mystery deepens, and we come closer to that difficult place where we must try to assume nothing.**"**

▲ **Korean Single Flower Vessel** | 2006
6 x 20⅞ x 6 inches (15 x 53 x 15 cm)
Slip-cast and hand-built porcelain; brass candleholder;
Marine Wudi and Xue Bai chicken-skin white glazes;
propane fired in reduction, cone 12
Photo by artist

◀ **Cup and Saucer Wall Sconce** | 2004
9 x 8¼ x 6¼ inches (23 x 21 x 16 cm)
Slip-cast porcelain; altered and fused; glazed
with Qingbai celadon; propane fired in
reduction, cone 12; raw brass with natural
patina, untreated
Photo by artist

Rose Tea Pot and Shadow | 2005 ▲

8¼ x 14½ inches (21 x 37 cm)
Carved porcelain; slip-cast spout and lid;
thrown and hand-built handles; hand-
built shadow with Morgan glaze, sgraffito
drawing; propane fired in reduction,
cone 12
Photo by artist

Menton Transfer | 2006 ▶

6¼ x 13 inches (16 x 33 cm)
Wheel-thrown, carved porcelain meiping;
slip-cast and carved shadow; HH qingbai
celadon and HH celadon (shadow) glazes;
propane fired in reduction, cone 13
Photo by artist

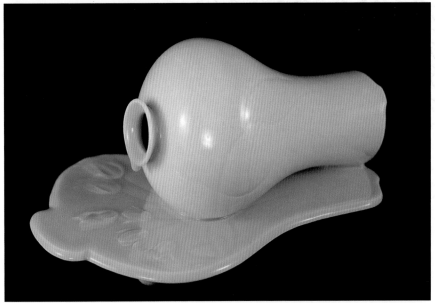

Leah Leitson

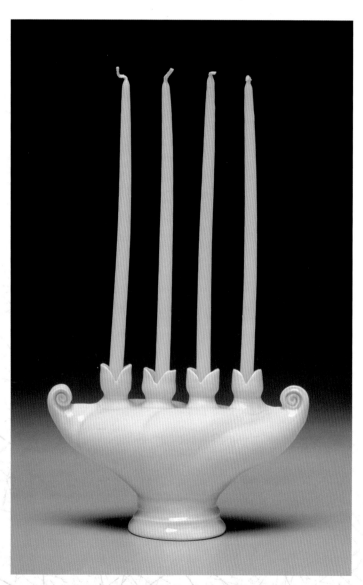

HANDLING HER PORCELAIN with a fluid delicacy, Leah Leitson creates forms that seem to flow from foot to rim in one easy movement. Often using salt-glaze to alter and soften the applied glazes, she sets up textured surfaces that direct the flow of the glaze. At times inspired by classical elements, at others working in a purely modernist vein, Leitson's vessels are always a visual and sensual delight.

◀ Candelabra | 2001
  5 x 9 x 3 inches (12.7 x 22.9 x 7.6 cm)
  Thrown and altered porcelain;
  oxidation fired, cone 6
  Photo by Tim Barnwell

▲ **Vase** | 2002

    11 x 4 x 4 inches (27.9 x 10.2 x 10.2 cm)
Thrown and altered porcelain; salt fired,
cone 10
Photo by Tim Barnwell

▲ **Pitcher** | 2006

    11 x 8 x 4½ inches (27.9 x 20.3 x 11.4 cm)
Wheel-thrown and altered porcelain; oxidation
fired, cone 6
Photo by Tim Barnwell

" I alter wheel-thrown components by pushing
in and out in a spiral fashion to give the pot
a sense of rhythm and to suggest organic
natural growth. For variation, I create lobes in
a vertical spiral too.**"**

▲ **Cup and Saucer** │ 1990
4 x 3 x 3½ inches (10.2 x 7.6 x 8.9 cm)
Porcelain; slip decorated; cone 10 reduction
Photo by artist

◀ **Ewer** │ 1992
9 x 3½ x 3½ inches
(22.9 x 8.9 x 8.9 cm)
Thrown and altered porcelain; salt
fired, cone 10
Photo by artist

LEAH

178

◀ **Lobed Sauce Boat** │ 1995

4 x 3½ x 5 inches
(10.2 x 8.9 x 12.7 cm)
Thrown and altered porcelain;
salt fired, cone 10
Photo by artist

Lobed Cruet Set │ 1996 ▶

6 x 5 x 3½ inches
(15.2 x 12.7 x 8.9 cm)
Thrown and altered
porcelain; salt fired,
cone 10
Photo by artist

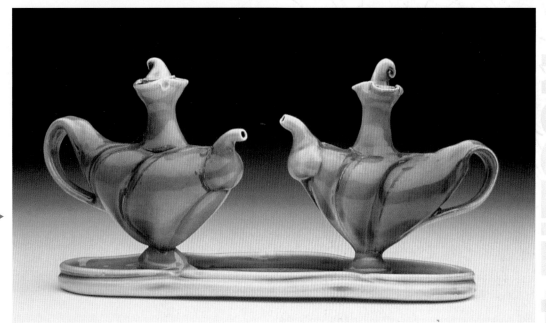

LEAH **LEITSON**

▲ **Place Setting** │ 2001

Platter: 11½ x 20 x 7½ (29.2 x 50.8 x 19 cm)
Thrown and altered porcelain; oxidation fired, cone 6
Photo by Tim Barnwell

" As a potter, I prefer to work in a series, which allows me to explore ideas and variations on a theme. This approach leads to a sureness and clarity that might be missed in a single attempt."

▲ **Breakfast Set** │ 2005

12½ x 24 x 9 (31.8 x 61 x 22.9 cm)
Thrown and altered porcelain;
oxidation fired, cone 6
Photo by Tim Barnwell

◀ **Oval Bowl** | 2002

4½ x 17 x 5½ inches
(11.4 x 43.2 x 14 cm)
Thrown and hand-built porcelain;
salt fired, cone 10
Photo by Tim Barnwell

▼ **Menorah** | 2000

Each: 2 x 2 x 1 inches
(51. X 5.1 x 2.5 cm)
Thrown and altered porcelain;
oxidation fired, cone 6
Photo by Tim Barnwell

" Combining historical references of the decorative arts with my own interpretation of nature results in work with a degree of elegance plus elements of play and whimsy. **"**

▲ Tulipiere | 2006

9 x 8 x 4½ inches (22.9 x 20.3 x 11.4 cm)
Thrown and altered porcelain; oxidation
fired, cone 6
Photo by Tim Barnwell

LEAH LEITSON

Keisuke Mizuno

DELICATELY BEAUTIFUL RECREATIONS of the natural forms created by Keisuke Mizuno bear closer inspection. Only then do the more subtle evidences of nature's life and death struggles become apparent. As one peers into Mizuno's work, seemingly perfect flowers floating on complexly glazed leaves give way to darker visions of slugs eating brown holes in an otherwise perfect representation of natural beauty.

Flemish vanitas painting often featured a skull surrounded by cut flowers and other objects, symbolizing the passage of time and the brevity of human life. Keisuke Mizuno's later works elaborate on this idea: human remains merge with flora and fauna, while insects devour the vegetation. The cycle of life is complete, the balance of nature revealed.

Mizuno's work has remarkable intricacy and requires infinite patience and dexterity. His ability to work with porcelain and overglaze enamels creates a familiar environment in which the viewer may contemplate Mizuno's challenging subject matter.

Forbidden Flower | 1999 ▶

    5 x 10 x 7 inches (12.7 x 25.4 x 17.8 cm)
Hand-built porcelain; glaze, china
paint; electric fired, cone 5
Photo by Craig Smith

Forbidden Fruit │ 1999 ▲

5 x 7 x 7 inches (12.7 x 17.8 x 17.8 cm)
Hand-built porcelain; glaze, china paint;
electric fired, cone 5
Photo by Craig Smith

Forbidden Fruit │ 1999 ▶

7 x 12 x 8 inches (17.8 x 30.5 x 20.3 cm)
Hand-built porcelain; glazd, china paint;
electric fired, cone 5
Photo by Dan Dennehy

"The Forbidden Flowers series holds images of death. Within their pistils and stamens, in the central areas of the flowers, are tiny skulls. In this way I draw you into the piece and then I've got a surprise for you."

▲ **Forbidden Flower** | 2001

5 ½ x 12 x 10 inches (14 x 30.5 x 25.4 cm)
Hand-built porcelain; glaze, china paint;
electric fired, cone 5
Photo by Anthony Cuñha

▲ **Forbidden Flower** | 2000

8 x 12 x 12 inches (20.3 x 30.5 x 30.5 cm)
Hand-built porcelain; glaze, china paint;
electric fired, cone 5
Photo by Anthony Cuñha

▲ **Forbidden Fruit** | 1999

5 x 10 x 7 inches (12.7 x 25.4 x 17.8 cm)
Hand-built porcelain; glaze, china paint;
electric fired, cone 5
Photo by Anthony Cuñha

◀ **Untitled** | 2004

5 x 5 x 8 inches (12.7 x 12.7 x 20.3 cm)
Hand-built porcelain; glaze, china paint;
electric fired, cone 5
Photo by Dan Dennehy

KEISUKE **MIZUNO**

" All of the transitions of life, from the embryonic stage to that of death and decay, are present in my work. I often use flowers or fruit as the essential element, a starting point for reflections on the transience of existence."

▲ **Forbidden Fruits** | 2000

6 x 12 x 10 inches (15.2 x 30.5 x 25.4 cm)
Hand-built porcelain; glaze, china paint;
electric fired, cone 5
Photo by Craig Smith

Purple Fruit
with the Balance | 2004 ▲

13 x 11 x 9 inches
(33 x 27.9 x 22.9 cm)
Hand-built porcelain; glaze,
china paint; electric fired, cone 5
Photo by Anthony Cuñha

Untitled | 2000 ▶

8 x 11 x 8 inches
(20.3 x 27.9 x 20.3 cm)
Hand-built porcelain; glaze,
china paint; electric fired, cone 5
Photo by Dan Dennehy

▲ **Untitled** | 2001

7 x 12 x 12 inches (17.8 x 30.5 x 30.5 cm)
Hand-built porcelain; glaze, china paint;
electric fired, cone 5
Photo by Anthony Cuñha

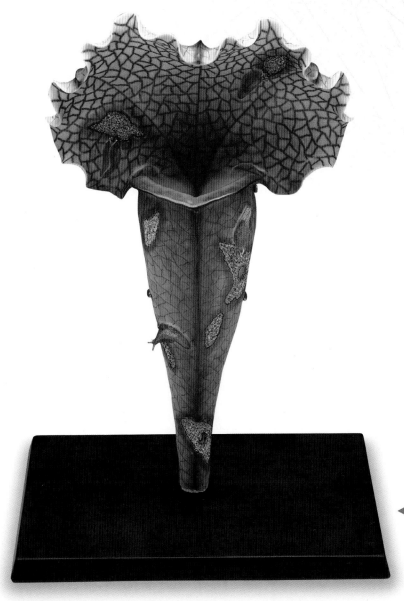

" I try to visualize a small portion of the complex intertwinement of visual disparity between life and death in nature—the intrinsic beauty of the transient nature of humanity. I carefully choose the materials and techniques that allow me to create a familiar and intimate environment for viewers to think about this difficult issue. "

◀ **Forbidden Flower** | 2001

14 x 8 x 6 inches (35.6 x 20.3 x 15.2 cm)
Hand-built porcelain; glaze, china paint; electric fired, cone 5
Photo by Dan Dennehy

KEISUKE **MIZUNO**

Sunkoo Yuh

THE COLORFUL, FIGURATIVE PORCELAIN SCULPTURES
by Sunkoo Yuh defy all expectations, both in scale and in the exuberant
diversity of images that crowd together into an
intense narrative. The playful figures populating his
work are simultaneously childlike and nightmarish,
qualities heightened by the freely applied, flowing
glazes. Glimpses of the long history of Eastern
ceramics appear frequently within the complexity of
the whole, along with cars, dogs, planes, high-rise
buildings, kitsch cartoon figures, corn on the cob, and
other images of modern life. Animals and birds often
are larger than humans, and primal images of various
types appear, sometimes in the form of macabre
masks. Scale is a fluid element in these forms, adding
to the fantastic element of Sunkoo Yuh's work.

Figure with Bird Hat | 1997 ▶
23 x 12 x 8 inches (58.4 x 30.5 x 20.3 cm)
Hand-built porcelain; glaze; gas fired in
oxidation, cone 10
Photo by artist

Marriage | 2005 ▶

24½ x 17 x 15 inches
(62.2 x 43.2 x 38.1 cm)
Hand-built porcelain;
cheesecloth; glaze; gas fired
in oxidation, cone 10
Photo by Larry Dean

▲ **Bedtime Story** │ 2002

27 x 20 x 17 inches (68.6 x 50.8 x 43.2 cm)
Hand-built porcelain; glaze; gas fired in oxidation,
cone 10
Photo by Larry Dean

▲ **Repatriation** │ 2001

51 x 28 x 22 inches (129.5 x 71.1 x 55.9 cm)
Hand-built porcelain; glaze; gas fired in oxidation,
cone 10
Photo by artist

" My works are built of different clay bodies and 50 different high-fire glazes on top of each other. Rather than controlling glazes, I allow them to play by their own rules, and I accept the results of unexpected serendipities."

▲ **I Want to See Your Smile** │ 2001

    29 x 18½ x 15 inches (73.7 x 47 x 38.1 cm)
    Hand-built porcelain; glaze; gas fired in
    oxidation, cone 10
    Photo by artist

▲ **Another Reflection** │ 2002

    26 x 16 x 13 inches (66 x 40.6 x 33 cm)
    Hand-built porcelain; glaze; gas fired in
    oxidation, cone 10
    Photo by Larry Dean

SUNKOO YUH

◀ **Anniversary** | 2003

25 x 13 x 11 inches (63.5 x 33 x 27.9 cm)
Hand-built porcelain; glaze; gas fired in oxidation,
cone 10
Photo by Larry Dean

Untitled | 2004 ▶

16½ x 15 x 15 inches (41.9 x 38.1 x 38.1 cm)
Hand-built porcelain; glaze; gas fired in
oxidation, cone 10
Photo by Larry Dean

" My work is a means of transforming interior images to tangible ceramic sculptures, sometimes monumental, sometimes small. Images that contain my unconscious concerns well up from inside me, and then I draw intuitively and spontaneously with ink and brush. I closely study these drawings and select a few to transform into three-dimensional clay sculptures. "

▲ **Memory of Pikesville, TN** | 2003

34 x 29 x 26 inches (86.4 x 73.7 x 66 cm)
Hand-built porcelain; glaze; gas fired in oxidation, cone 10
Photo by Larry Dean

SUNKOO YUH

" I have started to see universal issues, such as life and death, through my daughter's birth. I think I know now that everything can have both universal and personal meanings. Making art may be a quest in search of broad meanings or answers, but it can be expressed through small, mundane awareness of daily life."

▲ **Sacrific** | 2005

22 x 18 x 14 inches (55.9 x 45.7 x 35.6 cm)
Hand-built porcelain; glaze; gas fired in oxidation,
cone 10; gold luster, cone 018
Photos by Larry Dean

◀ **Ritual Cup** │ 1999

24 x 23 x 13 inches (61 x 58.4 x 33 cm)
Wheel-thrown and hand-built porcelain;
glaze; gas fired in oxidation, cone 10
Photo by artist

Welcome │ 2000 ▶

18 x 10 x 10 inches (45.7 x 25.4 x 25.4 cm)
Hand-built porcelain; glaze; gas fired in
oxidation, cone 10
Photo by artist

Edmund De Waal

ONE OF THE FOREMOST practitioners of a minimalist aesthetic in porcelain, Edmund De Waal works with seemingly simple thrown forms, usually in multiple variations. Through this multiplicity, he creates a much more complex work that often includes delicate subtleties of surface enhanced by the exquisite transparency of an icy blue-green celadon glaze. More recently working with color almost hidden inside site-specific installations, De Waal creates open forms that draw one in to investigate their interior space. Other groupings suggest landscapes. Still others play on the obsessive nature of collecting and categorization.

River | 2004 ▶

Largest:19¾ x 8¼ inches (50.2 x 21 cm)
Wheel-thrown porcelain; celadon glaze;
gas fired, cone 9
Photo by artist

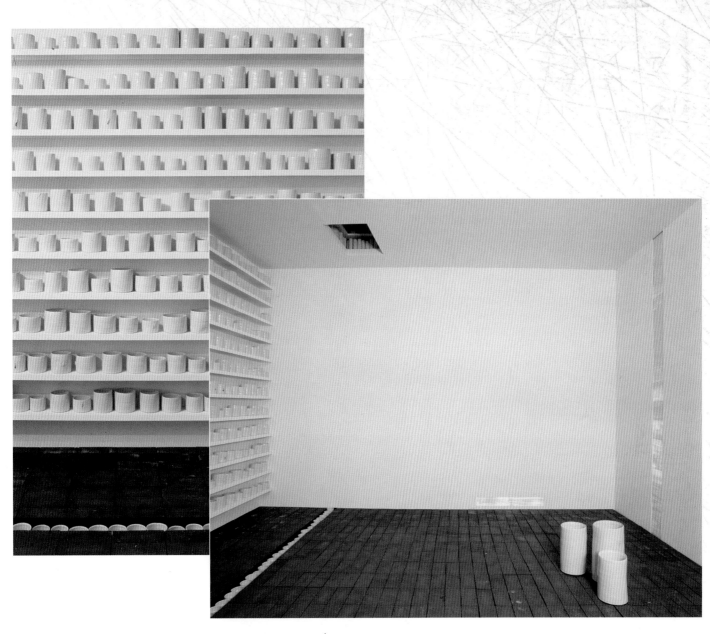

▲ Porcelain Room | 2003

Average: 6¼ x 4 inches (16 x 10 cm)
Wheel-thrown porcelain; celadon glaze; cone 9
Photos by artist

" Working in Japan has given me a feeling for how pots can work in the hand—how their heft, balance, and texture matter. My pots are slightly bashed and tell of their making. But working in Europe has given me a feeling for the ceramics of Modernism. So, my pots, though they are slightly crooked, aren't too gestural, aren't too domesticated."

▲ **Cup and Saucer** | 1995
Porcelain; celadon glaze
Photo by artist

Teapot | 2000 ▶
Porcelain; celadon glaze
Photo by artist

Below the Waterline | 2005

    2¾ x 4 inches (7 x 10.2 cm)
    Wheel-thrown porcelain; celadon
    glaze; gas fired, cone 9
    Photo by artist

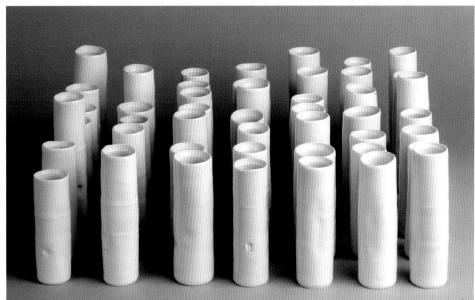

Sightless | 2005

    8 x 3½ inches (20.3 x 8.9 cm)
    Wheel-thrown porcelain; seven
    different white glazes; electric
    fired, cone 9
    Photo by artist

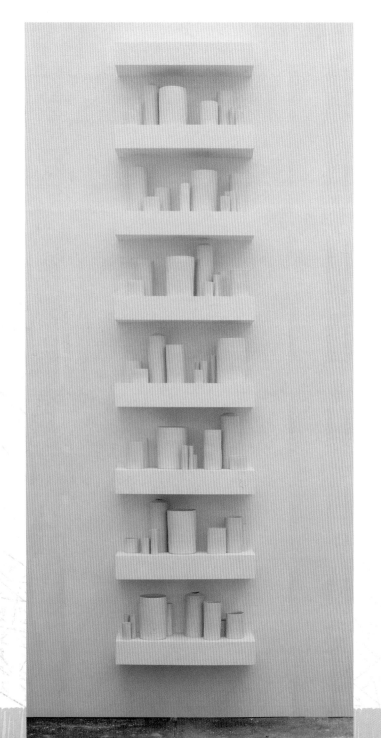

" Some years ago a friend lent me—for a day or two—a small, white porcelain cup. It dated from the very start of the 18th century and was made by Johann Friedrich Bottger, the alchemist-potter who formulated the first European porcelain body. The cup was a slight object, finely thrown, unmarked, with a slight chip in its rim. I loved it. It was completely singular, somewhere between a test object and a finished one, with a feeling of achievement about it. "

◀ Listing, Listing │ 2006

Largest: 10¾ x 4¼ inches (27.3 x 10.8 cm)
Wheel-thrown porcelain; white and celadon glazes;
oxidation and reduction fired, cone 8–9
Photo by artist

▲ **In a Dark Wood #2** | 2004

39½ x 6¼ inches (100 x 15.9 cm)
Wheel-thrown porcelain; celadon glaze;
gas fired, cone 9–10
Photo by artist

Tenebrae | 2004 ▶

8 x 10¾ (20.3 x 27.3 cm)
Wheel-thrown porcelain; oxidation;
tin glaze with colored glaze; cone 9
Photo by artist

◀ **Mendel's Shelf** │ 2004

6 x 6¼ inches (15.2 x 15.9 cm)
Wheel-thrown porcelain; white celadon glaze;
color glaze; oxidation fired, cone 9
Photo by artist

Day One │ 2003 ▶

8 x 6 inches (20.3 x 15.2 cm)
Wheel-thrown porcelain; white and colored
glazes; oxidation fired, cone 8
Photo by artist

" For the past 10 years I have been making installation groups, calling them "cargoes" of pots, an image that came from haunting images of sunken cargoes of porcelain. There are few images of groups of porcelain—we are much more used to seeing single pieces in isolated splendor.**"**

▲ **Porcelain Wall** │ 2006

2½ x 2 inches (6.4 x 5.1 cm)
Wheel-thrown porcelain; celadon glaze;
cone 9
Photos by artist

EDMUND DE WAAL

Gwyn Hanssen Pigott

WORKING WITHIN THE STILL-LIFE TRADITION,
Gwyn Hanssen Pigott throws porcelain vases, bowls, and
cups that she combines into arrangements that echo everyday
domestic situations and, at times, the landscape of life. With
strong references to nutrition coupled with survival, Pigott's
delicately thin and translucent porcelain
speaks of the fragility of life, its rhythms,
and even its expiration in works like Breath
and Fade. Her minimalist aesthetic is well
suited to porcelain in her use of simply
thrown forms, barely tweaked from their
geometric roots and glazed with ever-so-
subtle variations of transparent celadon-like
glazes.

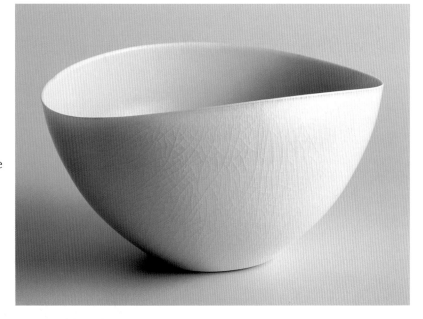

▲ Shell | 1999
4¼ x 8½ x 6½ inches (10.8 x 21.6 x 16.5 cm)
Limoges porcelain; glaze; wood fired, cone 10
Photo by Brian Hand

▲ **Still Life with Two Tall Beakers** │ 2004

10¼ x 11½ x 9¾ inches (26 x 29.2 x 24.8 cm)
Translucent porcelain; glaze; gas fired, cone 12
Photo by Brian Hand

▲ **Still Life with Bronze Cup** │ 1995

9¼ x 19⅞ x 6¼ inches
(23.5 x 50.5 x 16 cm)
Porcelain; glaze; wood fired, cone 11
Photo by Brian Hand

Pale Still Life │ 1992 ▶

9¾ x 8¼ x 6 inches
(24.8 x 21 x 15.2 cm)
Wheel-thrown porcelain; glaze;
wood fired, cone 11
Photo by John Thompson

" As a student of art history, I was intrigued and excited by some superb examples of Tang, Han, and Song Dynasty wares. But I was especially seduced by the fragile magic of the porcelains and the strange attraction of celadon glaze in its many forms. "

▲ Breath | 1999
   12 x 88¼ x 9¼ inches (30.5 x 224 x 23.5 cm)
   Porcelain; glaze; wood fired, cone 11
   Photo by Brian Hand

" The pots surprise me in their arrangements. I spend my time happily throwing, turning, glazing, and firing, before the special hours spent discovering the groupings of simplified shapes. Beakers, bowls, bottles, jugs, and teapots, by their relationships and placement, can become uncannily expressive of something other: a silence, an emotion, a thought. **"**

◀ **Silence** │ 1995

10¼ x 9 x 7¼ inches (26 x 22.9 x 18.4 cm)
Porcelain; glaze; wood fired, cone 11
Photo by Brian Hand

▼ **Yellow Still Life** │ 2003

6¾ x 18 x 6 inches (17.1 x 45.7 x 15.2 cm)
Translucent porcelain; glaze; gas fired,
cone 12
Photo by Brian Hand

Pale Still Life with Yellow Jug | 1994 ▶

  8 x 10½ x 9½ inches (20.3 x 26.8 x 24 cm)
  Porcelain; glaze; wood fired, cone 11
  Photo by Brian Hand

▼ **Yellow Teapot with Still Life** | 2002

  5¼ x 11 x 5¾ inches (13.3 x 27.9 x 14.6 cm)
  Limoges porcelain; glaze; gas fired, cone 11
  Photo by Brian Hand

▲ **Drift** | 2005

Largest: 11¾ x 59 x 9 inches (30 x 150 x 22.9 cm)
Translucent porcelain; glaze; gas fired, cone 12
Photo by Brian Hand

▲ **Fade** | 2003

Largest: 6½ x 43¼ x 6¾ inches (16.5 x 110 x 17.1 cm)
Translucent porcelain; glaze; gas fired, cone 12
Photo by Brian Hand

" I have been firing in higher temperatures recently for more translucence. I would like my work to be seen in windows. I love the way the colors change—how the seemingly simple and vulnerable pots become transformed by the light. "

▲ Chord | 2004

Largest: 7¼ x 38¾ x 6 inches (18.4 x 98.6 x 15.2 cm)
Translucent porcelain; glaze; gas fired, cone 12
Photo by Brian Hand

Kim Soo-Jeong

WITH THEIR CELADON glaze cloaking the porcelain's whiteness, Kim Soo-Jeong's vessels have a quiet resonance with the past. Clearly influenced by classical Korean pottery, Kim takes her work in subtle new directions through explorations of the lotus form in two and three dimensions. Her carving is exquisite and enhanced by a perfectly applied glaze. This frees the work from stiffness; it is very human, with a softness and variation that can only come from being made by hand.

▲ **Life** │ 2003

10¼ x 8 x 8¼ inches (26 x 20.3 x 21 cm)
Wheel-thrown porcelain; celadon
glazes; gas fired
Photo by artist

▲ **Life** | 1993

8¼ x 8¼ x 9 inches (21 x 21 x 22.9 cm)
Wheel-thrown porcelain; celadon
glaze; gas fired
Photo by artist

▲ **Life** | 1993

7 x 7 x 7¾ inches (17.8 x 17.8 x 19.7 cm)
Wheel-thrown porcelain; celadon glaze; gas fired
Photo by artist

Life | 1993 ▲

8¾ x 8¾ x 9 inches
(22.2 x 22.2 x 22.9 cm)
Wheel-thrown porcelain;
celadon glaze; gas fired
Photo by artist

Life | 1998 ▶

9¾ x 9¾ x 8¼ inches
(25 x 25 x 21 cm)
Wheel-thrown porcelain;
celadon glaze; gas fired
Photo by artist

" The most important aspect of my work relates to life's strength: the will to survive any darkness or difficulty that life holds for us. My work is about purity and life. **"**

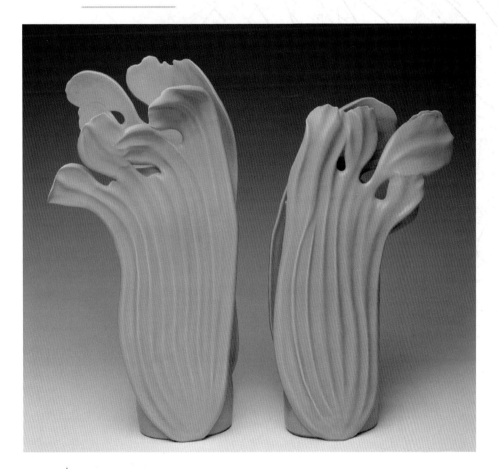

▲ **Life** | 1993

9¾ x 8¼ x 19 inches (24.8 x 21 x 48.3 cm)
Wheel-thrown and hand-built porcelain;
celadon glaze; gas fired
Photo by artist

" In the past, I used an oil-firing kiln. Today I fire my work in a gas kiln. Oil fuel gives a deep and calm celadon color while gas gives a more light and clear effect. "

▲ **Life** | 1998
6½ x 4¾ x 6½ inches (16.5 x 12 x 16.5 cm)
Wheel-thrown porcelain; celadon glazes; gas fired
Photo by artist

▲ **Life** | 1998
8¾ x 8¾ x 7¾ inches (22.2 x 22.2 x 19.7 cm)
Wheel-thrown porcelain; celadon and copper
glazes; gas fired
Photo by artist

▲ **Life** │ 2004

27 x 24¾ x 39¼ inches
(69 x 63 x 10 cm)
Wheel-thrown and hand-built
porcelain; celadon and copper glazes;
gas fired
Photo by artist

Life │ 2005 ▶

14¼ x 14¼ x 4½ inches
(36.2 x 36.2 x 11.4 cm)
Wheel-thrown porcelain; celadon
and copper glazes; gas fired
Photo by artist

" When I was a child, my father took me on a boat ride in a pond filled with lotus plants. Surrounded entirely by leaves and flowers, we couldn't see more than a few inches ahead of us. Here, my father set the standard of my life. He pointed to the muddy water and said that if my will was strong, I could maintain my pure spirit like those beautiful lotus flowers amidst the impurities of the world.**"**

▲ **Life** │ 2005
12 x 12 x 7½ inches (33 x 33 x 19 cm)
Wheel-thrown porcelain; celadon and copper glazes; gas fired
Photo by artist

▲ **Life** | 1996

5¼ x 5½ x 14¾ inches (13.3 x 14 x 37.5 cm)
Wheel-thrown and hand-built porcelain;
copper glaze; gas fired
Photo by artist

Matthew Metz

IN THE PROCESS of making contemporary porcelain wares, Matthew Metz uses a number of very traditional techniques: sgraffito, sprigging, slip inlay and carving, and vapor-glazing. His work borrows heavily from the ceramic history of Germany, England, and China, re-emerging with unique freshness. Many of his pieces use techniques similar to ancient Tz'u-chou pottery from China, such as applying thick black or brown slip to the entire surface before carving away the negative of the images to reveal a white background. Metz' imagery, however, more closely resembles 19th-century folk-art images from the United States than the floral carving of peonies and chrysanthemums typical of Tz'u-chou ware.

Flask | 2005 ▶

9 x 6 x 3 inches (23 x 15 x 7.5 cm)
Wheel-thrown porcelain;
sprigged and carved; glaze; wood
and oil fired with salt, cone 10
Photo by Peter Lee

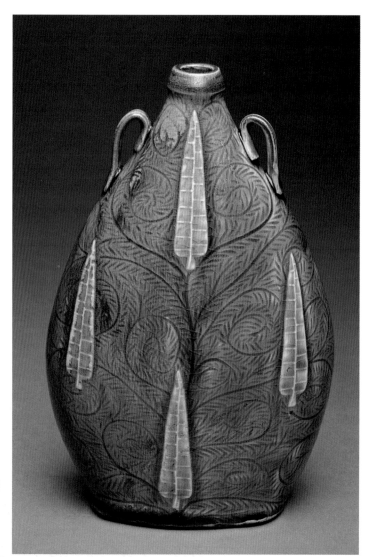

▲ Box | 2003

10 x 7 x 7 inches (25.5 x 18 x 18 cm)
Thrown and altered porcelain; sgraffito; wood and oil
fired with salt, cone 10
Photo by Peter Lee

Ewer | 1994 ▶

    4½ x 5 x 4 (11.5 x 12.5 x 10 cm)
Carved porcelain; glaze; wood
and oil fired, cone 10
Photo by artist

▼ **Ewers** | 1993

    5–7 inches (12.5–18 cm) in height
Porcelain; glaze; wood and oil fired
with salt, cone 10
Photo by artist

" Porcelain's whiteness heightens the contrast of my drawings, giving them the figure-ground look of woodcuts. The clay's fine texture allows me to work at the level of detail I want for sgraffito and sprigging. "

▲ **Cups** | 1998

Each: 4 x 3 x 3 inches
(10 x 7.5 x 7.5 cm)
Wheel-thrown porcelain; sprigged
and carved; glaze; wood and oil fired
with salt, cone 10
Photo by Peter Lee

Teapot | 1992 ▶

7 x 8 x 5 inches (18 x 20.5 x 12.5 cm)
Wheel-thrown porcelain; wood and
oil fired with salt, cone 10
Photo by artist

MATTHEW METZ

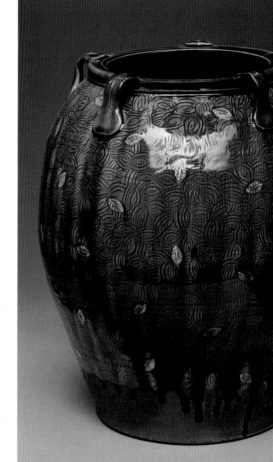

▲ Jar | 1990

20 x 16 x 16 inches (51 x 40.5 x 40.5 cm)
Porcelain; inlaid lines; gas fired with salt,
cone 10
Photo by artist

▲ Jar | 2004

24 x 16 x 16 inches (61 x 40.5 x 40.5 cm)
Wheel-thrown porcelain; sprigged and carved;
glaze; wood and oil fired with salt, cone 10
Photo by Peter Lee

" I spent a good part of my childhood in Indiana, pacing cornfields looking for arrowheads and other artifacts. Mere objects—the fact that they have been made and held by another human being in another time—can have power in a boy's imagination. My willingness to lose myself in the search for such small artifacts says a lot about the way I choose to work today."

▲ Platter | 2005

2 x 16 x 16 inches (5 x 40.5 x 40.5 cm)
Wheel-thrown porcelain; sgraffito; wood
and oil fired with salt, cone 10
Photo by Peter Lee

MATTHEW METZ

" Though my influences are eclectic (early American furniture and other decorative arts, Asian and Persian ceramics, woodcuts, embroidery, quilts, and folk art in general), I avoid ascribing direct narrative content to my imagery. Its primary function is decorative. "

▲ Plate | 2005

2 x 14 x 14 inches (5 x 35.5 x 35.5 cm)
Wheel-thrown porcelain; sgraffito; wood
and oil fired with salt, cone 10
Photo by Peter Lee

▲ **Box** | 2006

7 x 6 x 5 inches (18 x 15 x 12.5 cm)
Thrown and altered porcelain; sgraffito;
wood and oil fired with salt, cone 10
Photo by Peter Lee

▲ **Vase**, 2006

14 x 10 x 10 inches (35.5 x 25.5 x 25.5 cm)
Porcelain; wood and oil fired with salt, cone 10
Photo by Brian Oglesbee

Aysha Peltz

UNIQUE IN HER ABILITY to move porcelain in very fluid ways, Aysha Peltz alters wheel-thrown forms in ways that defy both the hard whiteness of fired porcelain, with their effortlessly liquid form, and also the technical difficulties of working on a large scale. Peltz found early on that she was more attracted to

the way thickly thrown porcelain moved, slumped, and cracked than in trying to achieve delicately thin porcelain pottery. Her mastery of faceting, altering, and distorting thrown forms is evident in these pots and perfectly complements her aesthetic reconnection of porcelain clay back to its natural form. Peltz uses flowing, softly colored glazes that break gently over carefully defined edges and textures to emphasize the subtleties of her surfaces. Her vessels at times echo architecture, the natural landscape, or the movement of water and wave, all the while carrying a sense of new growth and vital energy.

◀ **Salad Plate, Dessert Plate, and Cup** | 2006
Salad plate: 1 x 9 x 9 inches (2.5 x 22.9 x 22.9 cm);
dessert plate: 1 x 6 x 6 inches (2.5 x 15.2 x 15.2 cm);
cup: 6 x 3 x 3 inches (15.2 x 7.6 x 7.6 cm)
Wheel-thrown porcelain; glaze; propane fired in
oxidation, cone 10
Photo by Jeff Baird

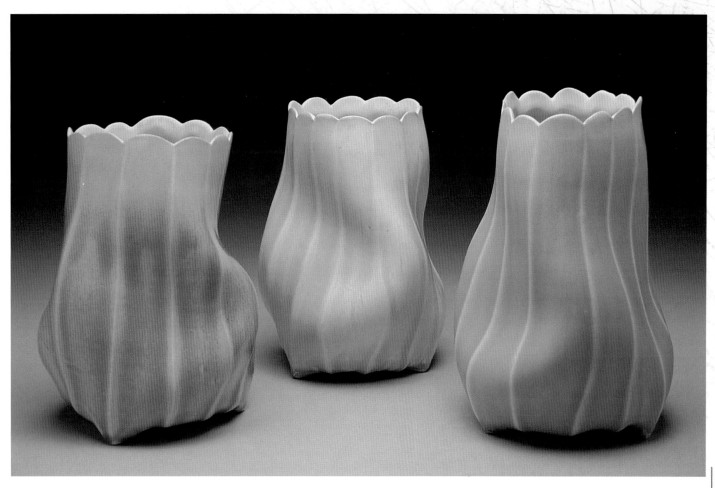

▲ **Three Faceted Vases** │ 2003

Each: 8 x 5 x 5 inches (20.3 x 12.7 x 12.7 cm)
Wheel-thrown and faceted porcelain; glaze;
propane fired in oxidation, cone 10
Photo by Todd Wahlstrom

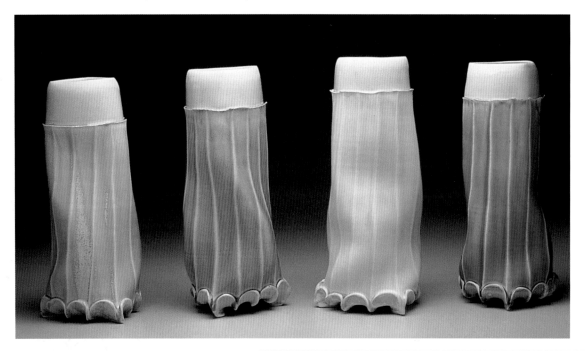

▲ **Four Vases** │ 2003

Each: 14 x 5 x 5 inches
(35.6 x 12.7 x 12.7 cm)
Wheel-thrown, faceted porcelain; glaze;
propane fired in oxidation, cone 10
Photo by Jeff Baird

Four Dinner Plates │ 2006 ▶

Each: 1 x 10½ x 10½ inches
(2.5 x 26.7 x 26.7 cm)
Wheel-thrown porcelain; glaze; propane
fired in oxidation, cone 10
Photo by Jeff Baird

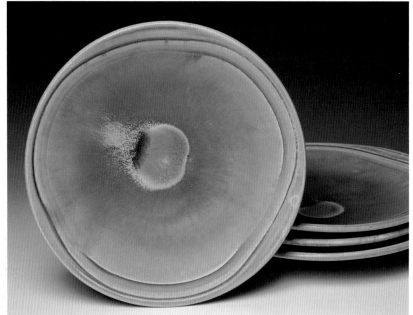

" The slumping, cracking, low volumes, and thick walls that occurred accidentally at first have become an important part of my form language today. Those early "failures" showed me a lot about what is essential in my attraction to porcelain.**"**

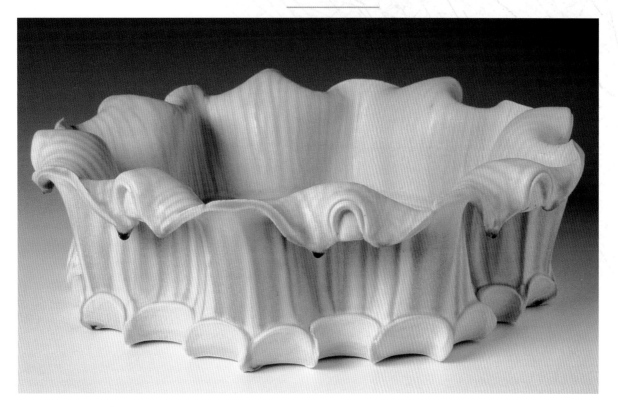

▲ Splash Bowl | 2004

4¾ x 13½ x 13½ inches (12 x 34.3 x 34.3 cm)
Wheel-thrown and altered porcelain; glaze; propane fired in
oxidation, cone 10
Photo by Jeff Baird

AYSHA

▲ **Lidded Jar** | 2005

13 x 11 x 11 inches (33 x 27.9 x 27.9 cm)
Wheel-thrown porcelain; glaze; propane fired
in oxidation, cone 10
Photo by Jeff Baird

▲ **Lidded Jar** | 2005

12 x 9 x 9 inches (30.5 x 22.9 x 22.9 cm)
Wheel-thrown porcelain; glaze; propane
fired in oxidation, cone 10
Photo by Jeff Baird

" Many of my current pots have become a landscape or terrain, a place where I can imagine and build a space. **"**

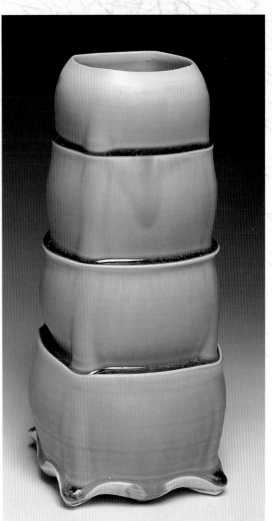

▲ **Lidded Jar** | 2004

10 x 9½ x 9½ inches (25.4 x 24.1 x 24.1 cm)
Wheel-thrown porcelain; glaze; propane
fired in oxidation, cone 10
Photo by Jeff Baird

▲ **Tiered Vase** | 2006

12 x 4 x 4 inches (30.5 x 10.2 x 10.2 cm)
Wheel-thrown porcelain; glaze; propane
fired in oxidation, cone 10
Photo by Jeff Baird

AYSHA PELTZ

▲ **Four Cups** | 2004

Each: 5½ x 3¼ inches (14 x 8.3 cm)
Wheel-thrown and faceted porcelain; glaze;
propane fired in oxidation, cone 10
Photo by Jeff Baird

◄ **Covered Jar** | 1995

7 x 5 x 5 inches (18 x 12.5 x 12.5 cm)
Wheel-thrown, faceted porcelain; celadon
glaze; reduction fired, cone 10
Photo by artist

" The challenge in making good work now does not involve a struggle with skill. As my hands have become more competent with working in porcelain, the challenge is to keep the sense of discovery and risk that so easily occurred in my beginning pots."

▲ **Lidded Jar** │ 2004

11 x 12 x 12 inches (27.9 x 30.5 x 30.5 cm)
Wheel-thrown porcelain; glaze; propane
fired in oxidation, cone 10
Photo by Jeff Baird

Linda Sikora

PORCELAIN SUPPORTS THE DELICACY of edge and intensity of glaze characteristic in Linda Sikora's work like no other clay could. Her use of polychrome glazes harks back to the Chinese, as do some elements in her forms. In other pieces, English and European whiteware influences appear. The fluidity of her glazes softens the crispness of tightly thrown forms. Sikora achieves a unique richness of surface through these decorative elements that makes the best of her ware glow—a quality made possible by the pure whiteness of the porcelain underneath it all.

Tureen and Stand | 2000 ▶

9 x 10 x 8 inches
(22.9 x 25.4 x 20.3 cm)
Wheel-thrown porcelain;
polychrome glaze; wood and
oil fired with salt, cone 10
Photo by Peter Lee

▲ **Ewer** │ 1998

    7 x 5½ x 4½ inches (17.8 x 14 x 11.4 cm)
    Wheel-thrown porcelain; polychrome glaze;
    wood and oil fired with salt, cone 10
    Photo by artist

◀ **Flower Vase in Fruit Bowl** │ 2005

    14 x 12 x 12 inches (35.6 x 30.5 x 30.5 cm)
    Wheel-thrown porcelain; polychrome glaze;
    wood and oil fired with salt, cone 10
    Photo by Brian Ogelsbee
    Courtesy of Ferrin Gallery

" Whether finishing a form with polychrome glaze or simply salting raw clay in an atmospheric kiln, I rely on porcelain. I find great pleasure in working with and coaxing porcelain into teapots, jars, bowls, and cups."

▲ **Eight Dishes** | 2005

Each: 2 x 5 x 5 inches (5.1 x 12.7 x 12.7 cm)
Wheel-thrown porcelain; polychrome glaze; wood
and oil fired with salt, cone 10
Photo by Peter Lee

▲ **Butter Dish** │ 1994

6 inches (15.2 cm) in height
Wheel-thrown porcelain;
wood and oil fired
with salt, cone 10
Photo by artist

◀ **Teapot** │ 2002

7 x 10½ x 6½ inches
(17.8 x 26.7 x 16.5 cm)
Wheel-thrown porcelain;
polychrome glaze; wood
and oil fired with salt,
cone 10
Photo by Peter Lee

LINDA SIKORA

▲ **Covered Jar** | 2001

12 x 10 x 10 inches (30.5 x 25.4 x 25.4 cm)
Wheel-thrown porcelain; polychrome glaze;
wood and oil fired with salt, cone 10
Photo by Peter Lee

▲ **Ewer** | 2001

8 x 5 x 4½ inches (20.3 x 12.7 x 11.4 cm)
Wheel-thrown porcelain; polychrome
glaze; wood and oil fired with salt, cone 10
Photo by Peter Lee

" My best pots have the capacity to move back and forth between the assertive and the peripheral within the visual and imaginative landscape. They foster both attention and inattention. I have always thought that pots, good pots, do not come to rest but continuously stir as they move back and forth between these states."

Covered Jar | 2003 ▶

16 x 11 x 11 inches (40.6 x 27.9 x 27.9 cm)
Wheel-thrown porcelain; polychrome glaze;
wood and oil fired with salt, cone 10
Photo by Peter Lee

LINDA SIKORA

" The legacy of porcelain's preciousness lingers on. Given this, porcelain can be strangely assertive, insisting on its own value, strength, a generous presentation of color, and a history of exclusivity."

▲ **Covered Jar** | 2002

14 x 11 x 11 inches (35.6 x 27.9 x 27.9 cm)
Wheel-thrown porcelain; polychrome
glaze; wood and oil fired with salt, cone 10
Photo by Peter Lee

Teapot, 2005 ▲

 5½ x 7 x 5½ inches
 (14 x 17.8 x 14 cm)
 Wheel-thrown porcelain;
 polychrome glaze; wood
 and oil fired with salt,
 cone 10
 Photo by Peter Lee

Teapot with Bail Handle | 2005 ▶

 7 x 7 x 5 inches (17.8 x 17.8 x 12.7 cm)
 Wheel-thrown porcelain; polychrome
 glaze; wood and oil fired with salt,
 cone 10
 Photo by Peter Lee

LINDA SIKORA

Kurt Weiser

THE OTHERWORLDLY, surreal images that Kurt Weiser paints on his vaguely classical Chinese jars are altered, as he says, "as if seen in a funhouse mirror." Weiser paints exquisite scenes over the entire surface with overglaze (china paint), making obvious reference to classical oil painting on flat surfaces, but in a dreamlike way. Nature and humans interact on these surfaces in lush Garden-of-Eden settings that carry a subtle ecological message. The soft curves of Weiser's porcelain forms interact with his applied imagery to create a fascinating interplay between two- and three-dimensional images. The resulting images have incredible depth and light.

Untitled | 1994 ▶
18 x 12 inches (45.5 x 30.5 cm)
Slip-cast porcelain; electric fired,
cone 10; luster, cone 018
Photo by artist

▲ **Naturalist** | 2001

12 x 13 inches (30.5 x 33 cm)
Slip-cast porcelain; electric fired, cone 10; luster, cone 018
Photo by artist

"For years, I had the vague feeling that the best expression of porcelain only came as a gift of nature, until I realized the materials are there to allow you to say what you need to say, not to tell you what to say. So I gave up trying to control nature and decided to use what I had learned about the materials to express some ideas about nature itself and my place in it."

▲ **Roulette** │ 2001

15 x 17 inches (38 x 43 cm)
Slip-cast porcelain; electric fired, cone 10; luster, cone 018
Photo by artist

▲ **Perfume** │ 2002

  19 x 12 inches (48.5 x 30.5 cm)
  Slip-cast porcelain; electric fired,
  cone 10; luster, cone 018
  Photo by artist

▲ **Chihuahua** │ 2002

  19½ x 10½ inches (49.5 x 26.5 cm)
  Slip-cast porcelain; electric fired,
  cone 10; luster, cone 018
  Photo by artist

▲ **Navigator** | 2002

11 x 16½ inches (28 x 42 cm)
Slip-cast porcelain; electric fired,
cone 10; luster, cone 018
Photo by artist

▲ **Fidelity** | 2003

19 x 13 inches (48.5 x 33 cm)
Slip-cast porcelain; electric fired,
cone 10; luster, cone 018
Photo by artist

"I started drawing and painting on pots out of desperation more than anything else—to have some say over what happened on the surface.**"**

▲ **Semi-Conscious** │ 2004

    13½ x 14 inches (34.5 x 35.5 cm)
    Slip-cast porcelain; electric fired, cone 10; luster, cone 018
    Photo by artist

"The ideas and subjects of my paintings on the pots are for the most part just a collection of my own history of fantasy and view of reality, built the same way we dream. A central idea and a cast of other characters and environments just seem to show up to complete the picture."

▲ Green Cup │ 2005

11½ x 12½ inches (29 x 32 cm)
Slip-cast porcelain; electric fired,
cone 10; luster, cone 018
Photo by artist

◄ Outdoor Life │ 2000

12 x 12 inches (30.5 x 30.5 cm)
Slip-cast porcelain; electric fired, cone 10;
luster, cone 018
Photo by artist

▲ **Abduction Jar** | 1999

18 x 11 inches (45.5 x 28 cm)
Slip-cast porcelain; electric fired, cone 10;
luster, cone 018
Photo by artist

▲ **Cancasia** | 2003

16½ x 12 inches (42 x 30.5 cm)
Slip-cast porcelain; electric fired,
con e 10; luster, cone 018
Photo by artist

Edward S. Eberle

ALTHOUGH HE RECENTLY STARTED MAKING work from raw, unglazed thrown forms, Edward Eberle is best known for his architecturally influenced porcelain forms, upon which he draws complex narratives. These delicately drawn and classically inspired images of pure black terra sigillata on stark white unglazed porcelain build, churn, and overlay on the clay's surfaces, engrossing the viewer with a rich visual tapestry of figures. Images, once drawn and now partly erased, peek between the hard blackness of the final images in ghostly grays.

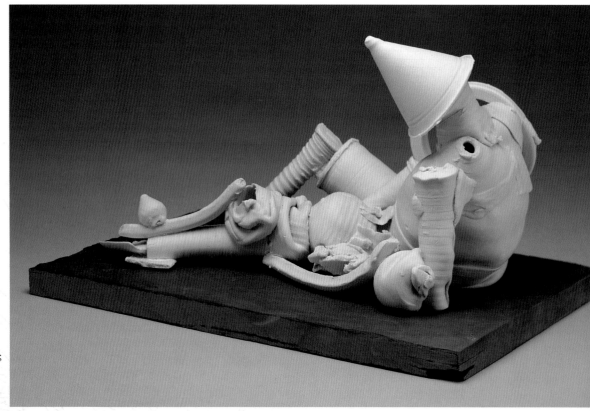

The Jester | 2004 ▶
6 x 7½ x 10½ inches
(15.2 x 19 x 26.7 cm)
Wheel-thrown porcelain;
terra sigillata; reduction
fired, cone 9–10; slate
Photo by Jonathan P.C. Eberle

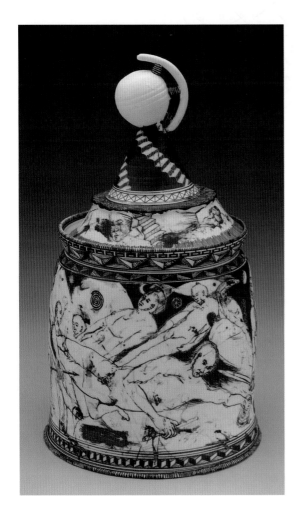

▲ **Hermetic Crown II** | 1991

11¼ x 6½ x 6½ inches
(28.6 x 16.5 x 16.5 cm)
Wheel-thrown porcelain; terra sigillata;
reduction fired, cone 9–10
Photo by John White

▲ **Ship–Demonstrative Teapot** 1991

6½ x 5½ x 7 inches (16.5 x 14 x 17.8 cm)
Wheel-thrown porcelain; terra sigillata; reduction fired,
cone 9–10; gold leaf
Photo by artist

▲ **Hermetic Crown II** │ 1991

11¼ x 6½ x 6½ inches (28.6 x 16.5 x 16.5 cm)
Wheel-thrown porcelain; terra sigillata;
reduction fired, cone 9–10
Photo by John White

▲ **Artist with Obscure Forms** │ 2001

2½ x 18 x 18 inches (6.5 x 45.7 x 45.7 cm)
Wheel-thrown porcelain; terra sigillata; reduction
fired, cone 9–10
Photo by artist

"Something special, poetical, and alchemical resides in the simplicity of terra sigillata on porcelain—a melding of like materials. Clay meets clay to become one in the fire."

▲ Twenty-Five Years to Bachelard | 1995

18 x 12 x 8 inches (25.5 x 30.5 x 20.3 cm)
Wheel-thrown porcelain; terra sigillata; reduction fired,
cone 9–10; gold leaf
Photo by artist

▲ Active Nurturing | 1991

3 x 9 x 9 inches (7.5 x 23 x 23 cm)
Wheel-thrown porcelain; terra sigillata;
reduction fired, cone 9–10
Photo by artist

EDWARD EBERLE

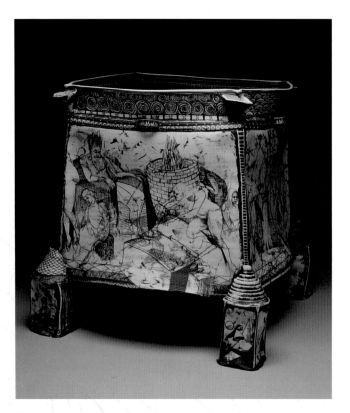

▲ **The Crown, the Screen, the Fire, the Dream** │ 1995

    13 x 13½ x 13 inches (33 x 34.3 x 33 cm)
Wheel-thrown porcelain; terra sigillata;
reduction fired, cone 9–10
Photo by artist

▲ **The Grass Will Grow Again** │ 1994

    18 x 16 x 16 inches (45.7 x 40.5 x 40.5 cm)
Wheel-thrown porcelain; terra sigillata;
reduction fired, cone 9–10
Photo by artist

"Intuition is my driving force."

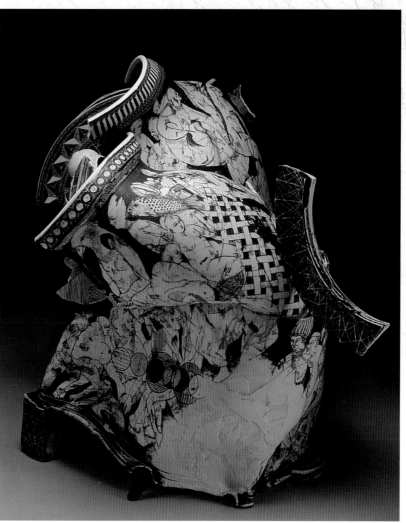

Sidestep | 2000 ▶

19 x 19 x 17 inches
(48.3 x 48.3 x 43.2 cm)
Wheel-thrown porcelain;
terra sigillata; reduction fired,
cone 9–10
Photos by artist

"My clay of choice is porcelain because it suits me and suits my needs. Porcelain is my own prima materia. I respond to its sensitivity and plasticity, its feel and responsiveness, and in particular to its clarity of surface, form, and color."

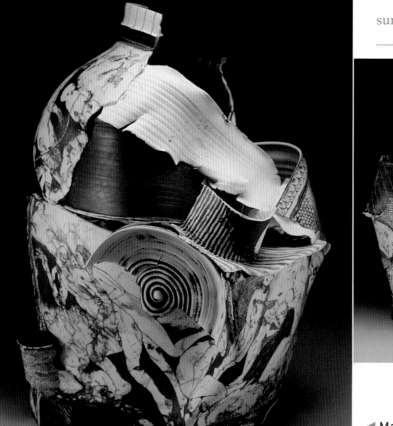

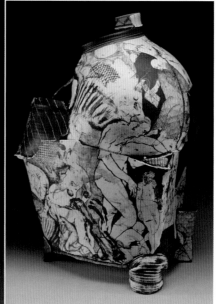

◀ **Man on a Plane** | 1999
18¼ x 14½ x 12 inches (46.5 x 36.8 x 30.5 cm)
Wheel-thrown porcelain; terra sigillata; reduction fired, cone 9–10
Photos by artist

▲ **First Facet** | 1998

26 x 16 x 16 inches (66 x 40.5 x 40.5 cm)
Wheel-thrown porcelain; terra sigillata;
reduction fired, cone 9–10; gold leaf
Photo by artist

▲ **The Sentinel** | 1995

17 x 16 x 16 inches (43.2 x 40.5 x 40.5 cm)
Wheel-thrown porcelain; terra sigillata;
reduction fired, cone 9–10; gold leaf
Photo by artist

Silvie Granatelli

CELEBRATING FOOD with her functional porcelain, Silvie Granatelli is interested in the interaction between a particular culinary dish and her pottery, often making work for a specific recipe. Her pottery shows influences from classical Italian ceramics to natural forms, as in her swan-handled cream pitchers. Her command of porcelain is evident in these altered forms, which move fluidly from round to square to oval.

▲ **Ruffled Edge Moon Bowl** | 2004

10 x 10 x 6 inches (25.5 x 25.5 x 15 cm)
Wheel-thrown and hand-built porcelain; crystal matte and black glazes; gas fired, cone 10
Photo by Tim Barnwell

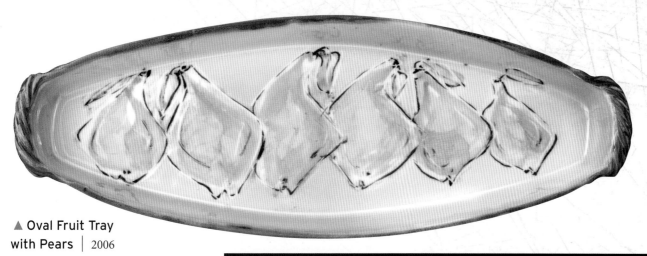

▲ **Oval Fruit Tray**
with Pears | 2006

2 x 18 x 8 inches (5 x 45.5 x 20.5 cm)
Slip-cast porcelain; stain and clear
glaze; gas fired, cone 10
Photo by Molly Selznick

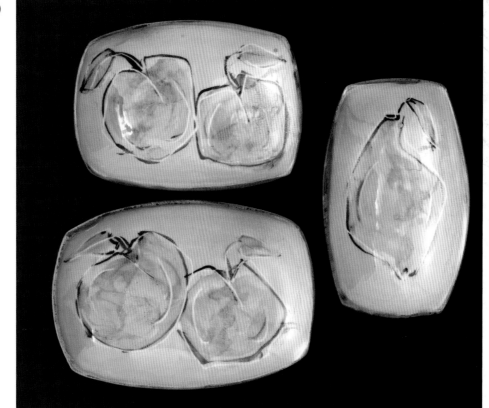

Shallow Fruit
Serving Bowls | 2006 ▶

Bottom dish: 2½ x 5 x 4 inches
(6.5 x 12.7 x 10.2 cm)
Drape mold porcelain; thrown foot;
stain, clear and matte glazes with
latex resist; gas fired, cone 10
Photo by Molly Selznick

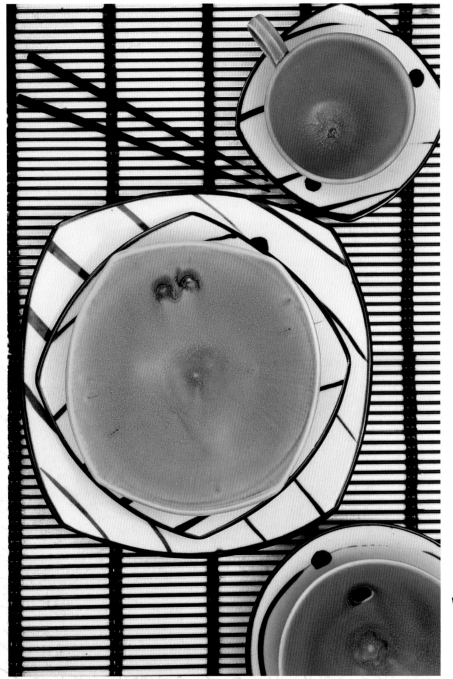

"I think of the pot as body and seek to find ways to subtly refer to several aspects of our human need to embellish our bodies; for example, by making the inside of pots wet-looking while the outsides have a matte finish. The textured surfaces of my pots make reference to cultures that use tattoo and scarification to enhance the skin and change the form of the body."

◀ **Stripe/Square Dinnerware** | 1989

1½ x 10 x 10 inches (4 x 25.5 x 25.5 cm)
Wheel-thrown and cut porcelain; clear glaze over black stain; matte turquoise glaze; gas fired, cone 10
Photo by Al Knuckols

Wavy Edge Dinnerware | 2006 ▶

1½ x 10 x 10 inches (4 x 25.5 x 25.5 cm)
Wheel-thrown and cut porcelain; matte glaze; gas fired, cone 10
Photo by Molly Selznick

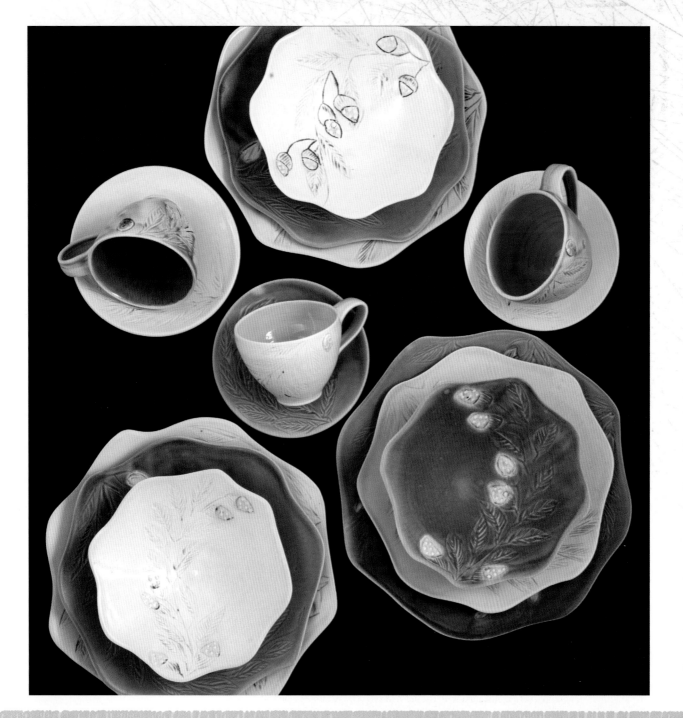

▲ **Swan Cream Pitchers** | 2006

4 x 6 x 3½ inches (10 x 15 x 9 cm)
Wheel-thrown porcelain; bottom trimmed; hand-built handles; glaze; gas fired, cone 10
Photo by Molly Selznick

Crystaline Glaze Serving Bowl | 2006 ▶

10 x 12 x 12 inches
(25.5 x 30.5 x 30.5 cm)
Wheel-thrown porcelain; crystalline matte glaze; gas fired, cone 10
Photo by Molly Selznick

SILVIE

▲ **Darted Pitcher** | 2003

    8 x 7 x 4 inches (20.5 x 18 x 10 cm)
    Wheel-thrown, altered, and hand-carved porcelain;
    matte and glossy turquoise glazes; gas fired, cone 10
    Photo by Tim Barnwell

◀ **Etruscan Inspired Pitcher** | 2004

    12 x 7 x 5 inches (30.5 x 18 x 12.5 cm)
    Wheel-thrown porcelain; crystal matte and black
    glazes; gas fired, cone 10
    Photo by Tim Barnwell

"How and what we eat are means by which society creates itself and acts out its aims. My pots were inspired by various food trends throughout the decades of my life. Making pots that follow what American culture is eating gives me a way to understand that milieu."

◀ **Lunch and Breakfast Sets** | 2006

1 x 8 x 7 inches
(2.5 x 20.5 x 18 cm)
Slip-cast porcelain;
carved and decorated;
glazed with latex resist;
gas fired, cone 10
Photo by Molly Selznick

Fluted Tea Bowl | 2006 ▶

5 x 3 x 3 inches (12.5 x 7.5 x 7.5 cm)
Wheel-thrown and fluted porcelain;
crystalline matte and black glazes;
gas fired, cone 10
Photo by Molly Selznick

Bird Box ▼

4½ x 5 x 3½ inches (11.5 x 12.5 x 9 cm)
Wheel-thrown, hand-built, and altered
porcelain; sprigged and cut birds; box:
matt glaze, birds: glossy glaze; gas fired,
cone 10
Photo by Tim Barnwell

Nicholas Homoky

THE WHITENESS OF PORCELAIN acts as a canvas on Nicholas Homoky's playful forms. Rather than impose incongruous images on his pieces, Homoky's crisp line drawings in black seem to extend, dissect, and analyze the forms upon which they are drawn. In an often brilliant interplay between two and three dimensions, his vessels with drawings cause us to consider more than the otherwise straightforward usefulness of many of these pots.

▲ **From a Drawing** | 2002

4½ x 9¾ x 5¼ inches (11.4 x 24.8 x 13.3 cm)
Wheel-thrown and slab-built porcelain, turned; carved, inlaid;
oxidation fired to 1260°F (682° C), cone 8; hand polished
Photo by artist

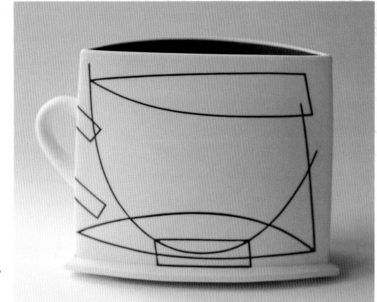

Cup With a Drawing │ 2003 ▶

5¼ x 6¼ x 2¾ inches
(13.3 x 15.9 x 7 cm)
Wheel-thrown porcelain, cut,
reassembled; carved, inlaid
drawing; unglazed; electric fired,
cone 8
Photo by artist

Porcelain Mug │ 1981 ▶

6 x 8¼ x 7 inches
(15.2 x 21 x 17.8 cm)
Wheel-thrown, turned porcelain; engraved, inlaid drawing,
painted with slip; unglazed;
electric fired, cone 8
Photo by artist

"Working with
essentially two
materials, pure white
porcelain and black
slip, allowed me to
be playful, creative,
and inventive
within self-imposed
limitations.**"**

▲ Bowl with a Tube | 2003
4 x 7 x 4 inches
(10.2 x 17.8 x 10.2 cm)
Wheel-thrown porcelain; painted,
unglazed; electric fired, cone 8
Photos by artist

Here and There | 2002 ▶

3¼ x 5¾ x 6¾ inches
(8.3 x 14.6 x 17.1 cm)
Wheel-thrown, turned
porcelain; painted slip; unglazed; electric fired, cone 8
Photo by artist

▼ Vessel with Bent Tubes | 2002

4¼ x 13½ x 3½ inches
(10.8 x 34.3 x 8.9 cm)
Wheel-thrown porcelain; carved,
painted, inlaid slip; unglazed;
electric fired, cone 8
Photo by artist

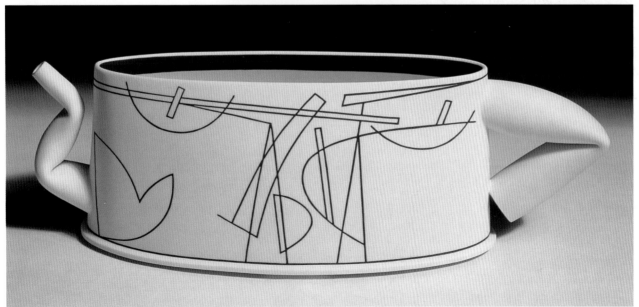

▲ **Graphic Teapot** | 1983

4¼ x 5½ x 3¼ inches (10.8 x 14 x 8.3 cm)
Wheel-thrown and slab-built porcelain; tubes thrown
on a stick; engraved drawings inlaid, painted with slip;
unglazed; electric fired, cone 8
Photo by artist

▲ **Teapot Drawing** | 1980

5½ x 4¼ x 1½ inches (14 x 10.8 x 3.8 cm)
Hand-built porcelain; engraved drawing, inlaid with slip;
unglazed; electric fired, cone 8
Photo by artist

"I was born number four in an eventual brood of six. Everything I had was secondhand and had to be shared with my siblings. As a consequence of having nothing of my own, I became driven to make the most of the simple and ordinary things in my environment. My sense of security was established in the realm of making things, of being resourceful, of making something of value from nothing."

Small Double Teapot | 1987 ▶

6 x 5¼ x 4¼ inches
(15.2 x 13.3 x 10.8 cm)
Wheel-thrown porcelain; engraved
drawings with inlaid, painted slip;
unglazed; electric fired, cone 8
Photo by artist

NICHOLAS TOMOKY

"I followed the idea of making vessels, not as pottery, but as three-dimensional drawings. To me, a thrown vessel is a drawing. Edges and shadows are part of my extended idea of what a drawing is. Add to this the fact that clay can be drawn on, and it explains the beginning of my work with black slip and white porcelain."

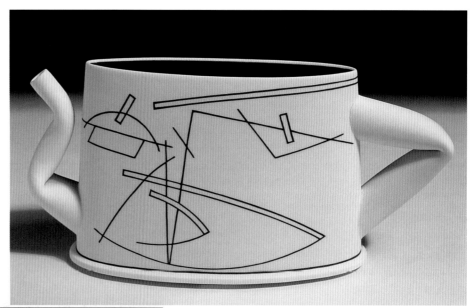

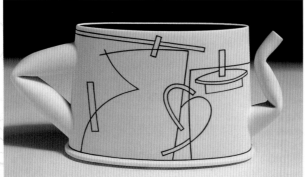

▲ **Playful Tea** │ 2002

4¾ x 9¾ x 3¼ inches (12 x 24.8 x 8.3 cm)
Wheel-thrown, slabbed porcelain; tubes rolled on a stick; painted, inlaid engraving; unglazed; electric fired to 1260°F (682° C), cone 8
Photos by artist

Teapot | 1997 ▶

4¼ x 8¼ inches (10.8 x 21 cm)
Wheel-thrown, cut, reassembled
porcelain; tubes rolled on a stick;
engraved drawing, inlaid and
painted slip; electric fired, cone 8
Photo by artist

◀ **Porcelain Drawing** | 1990

6¼ x 5¼ x 3½ inches
(15.9 x 13.3 x 8.9 cm)
Wheel-thrown and slab-built porcelain; engraved drawing with slip,
painting, inlay; unglazed; electric
fired, cone 08
Photo by artist

Taizo Kuroda

WORKING WITH THE PURE WHITENESS of porcelain, Taizo Kuroda throws pottery with a highly refined surface and a delicately casual air in rims that sag gently and occasionally ripple or tear. Kuroda pushes the wet porcelain to amazing thinness, knowing just when to stop to achieve maximum tension between the tightly thrown shapes and their gracefully active edges. His work is completely about porcelain the material in many ways, but it's also very much about the process of making by hand. It is work that could be cold and stark, but is enlivened by Kuroda's sensitive touch.

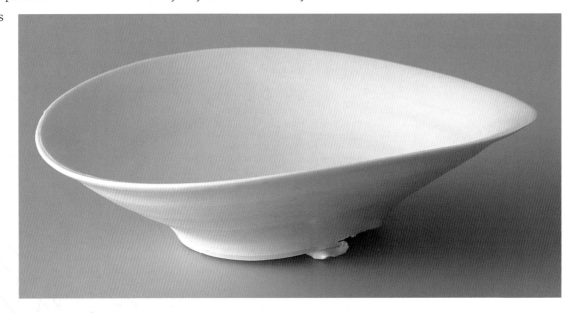

▲ **Untitled** │ 1999

7½ x 2¾ inches (19 x 7 cm)
Wheel-thrown New Zealand and Japanese Arita kaolins, mixed;
unglazed; electric kiln fired, cone 2318°F (1270°C)
Photo by Masanobu Fukuda

"My mind seems to be made up around three things: the color white, a vessel, and the wheel. To me, white porcelain is not just a matter of style, but the medium I use to discover truth.**"**

◀ **Untitled** │ 1999
7⅞ x 14¼ inches (20 x 36 cm)
Wheel-thrown New Zealand and
Japanese Arita kaolins, mixed;
unglazed; electric kiln fired, cone
2318°F (1270°C)
Photo by Masanobu Fukuda

"Since I began making white porcelain, I took to making pieces with very thin edges. This leads people to assume that I am using a high-speed wheel. The reverse is true. I make my wheel spin very slowly. One's concentration is greatly enhanced when time passes slowly, and the movement of the hand becomes more expressive."

Untitled | 1987–1988 ▶

Top: 5⅛ x 11¾ x 4¼ inches (13 x 30 x 11 cm); center: 6¼ x 6¾ x 5⅛ inches (16 x 17 x 13 cm); bottom: 4¼ x 8¼ x 3½ inches (11 x 21 x 9 cm)
Wheel-thrown New Zealand and Japanese Arita kaolins, mixed; unglazed; electric kiln fired, cone 2318°F (1270°C)
Photo by Masanobu Fukuda

▲ Untitled | 1999

7½ x 2¾ inches (19 x 7 cm)
Wheel-thrown New Zealand and
Japanese Arita kaolins, mixed;
unglazed; electric kiln fired, cone
2318°F (1270°C)
Photo by Masanobu Fukuda

Untitled | 1999 ▶

4¾ x 11¾ inches (12 x 30 cm)
Wheel-thrown New Zealand and
Japanese Arita kaolins, mixed;
unglazed; electric kiln fired, cone
2318°F (1270°C)
Photo by Masanobu Fukuda

TAIZO KURODA

"If you create something, you have to be sure that people are going to understand it. You can do that with words, but I use white porcelain instead. When I make a piece of pottery, it becomes a motif—a word. And that word is midway between yes and no."

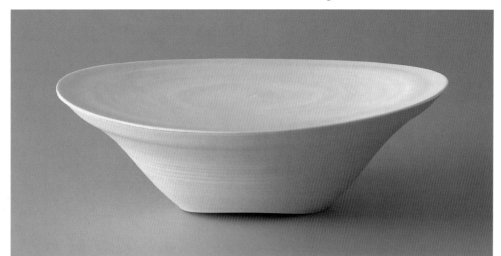

◀ **Untitled** │ 1999
9 x 3⅜ inches (23 x 8.5 cm)
Wheel-thrown New Zealand and
Japanese Arita kaolins, mixed;
unglazed; electric kiln fired, cone
2318°F (1270°C)
Photo by Masanobu Fukuda

◀ **Untitled** │ 1999
6¾ x 2¾ inches (17 x 7 cm)
Wheel-thrown New Zealand and
Japanese Arita kaolins, mixed;
unglazed; electric kiln fired, cone
2318°F (1270°C)
Photo by Masanobu Fukuda

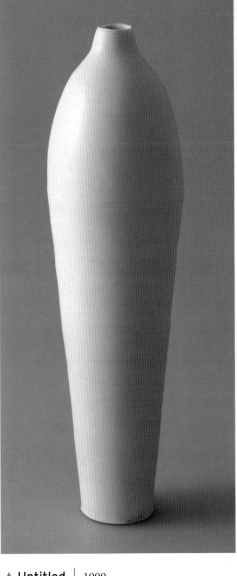

▲ **Untitled** | 1999

4¾ x 15¾ inches (12 x 40 cm)
Wheel-thrown New Zealand and Japanese
Arita kaolins, mixed; unglazed; electric
kiln fired, cone 2318°F (1270°C)
Photo by Masanobu Fukuda

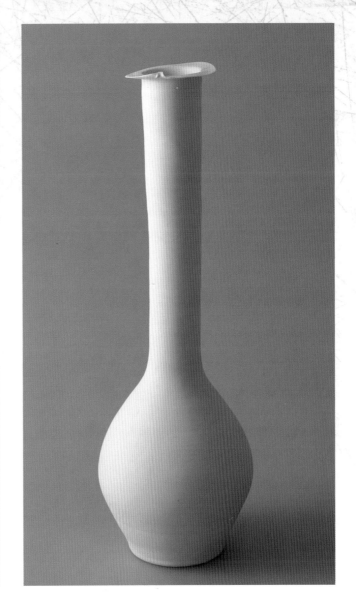

▲ **Untitled** | 1999

4¾ x 17¾ inches (12 x 45 cm)
Wheel-thrown New Zealand and Japanese
Arita kaolins, mixed; unglazed; electric kiln
fired, cone 2318°F (1270°C)
Photo by Masanobu Fukuda

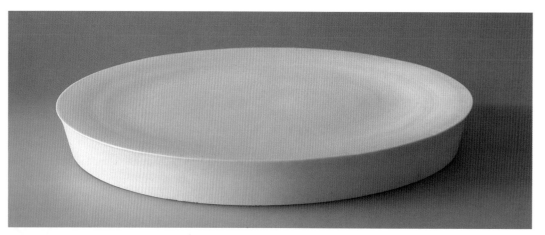

▲ Untitled | 1999
1¼ x 12 inches (3.2 x 30 cm)
Wheel-thrown New Zealand and
Japanese Arita kaolins, mixed;
unglazed; electric kiln fired, cone
2318°F (1270°C)
Photo by Masanobu Fukuda

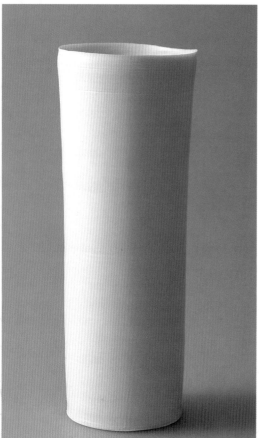

◄ Untitled | 1999
3½ x 9¾ inches (9 x 25 cm)
Wheel-thrown New Zealand and
Japanese Arita kaolins, mixed;
unglazed; electric kiln fired,
cone 2318°F (1270°C)
Photo by Masanobu Fukuda

"I like simple, ordinary things, and I only wish I could make something really and truly ordinary. But if I try to do so, it turns out otherwise. I think this is true of everyone; it isn't so easy to make ordinary things.**"**

▲ Untitled │ 1999

Each: 2¾ x 2 inches (7 x 5.1 cm)
Wheel-thrown New Zealand and Japanese Arita
kaolins, mixed; unglazed white porcelain; electric
kiln fired, cone 2318°F (1270°C)
Photo by Masanobu Fukuda

Prue Venables

THE GRACEFUL, OFTEN DELICATELY PIERCED porcelain forms by Australian Prue Venables hover somewhere between the functional and sculptural in their clean, strong form. Her sensitive altering of round, wheel-thrown pots creates a quiet elliptical tension between round and oval. Seemingly derived from industrial and chemical porcelain shapes, her work retains a hand-friendly scale and a sense of wanting to be used, even though we're not always sure for what purpose. Such a dialogue between artist and viewer gives Venables' work a critical edginess.

▲ **White Oval Scoop, Pierced; White Oval Spoon, Pierced** | 2005
Scoop: 5¼ x 11½ x 7½ inches (13.3 x 29.2 x 19 cm);
spoon: 11¾ x 3½ x 3¼ inches (30 x 8.9 x 8.3 cm)
Hand-thrown and altered porcelain, new base added to scoop;
pierced; calcium glaze; gas fired in reduction, cone 12
Photo by Terence Bogue

▲ **Tea Set on Black Tray** | 2002

Tray: 4¾ x 19 x 16¾ (12 x 48.3 x 41.3 cm); teapot: 9¾ x
9½ x 5¼ inches (24.8 x 24.1 x 13.3 cm)
Hand-thrown and altered porcelain, new base added;
gas fired in reduction, cone 12
Photo by Terence Bogue

▲ **Oval Dish and Oval Jug, Black and Aubergine** | 2005

Dish: 4 x 6¾ x 5¼ inches (10.2 x 17.1 x 13.3 cm);
jug: 4 x 2¼ x 1½ inches (10.2 x 5.7 x 3.8 cm)
Hand-thrown and altered porcelain, new base added;
gas fired in reduction, cone 12; calcium glaze
Photo by Terence Bogue

*"*I decided to move away
from the soft fragility of
earthenware and toward
the clear, hard, ringing
translucency of porcelain.
Motivated by my search for
simplicity and refinement,
fresh approaches to making
emerged, and new and
more challenging forms
developed. *"*

Ladle, Pierced | 2003 ▶

11¾ x 2¾ x 3½ inches (30 x 7 x 8.9 cm)
Hand-thrown and altered porcelain,
pierced; fired on rim, gas fired in
reduction, cone 12; calcium glaze
Photo by Terence Bogue

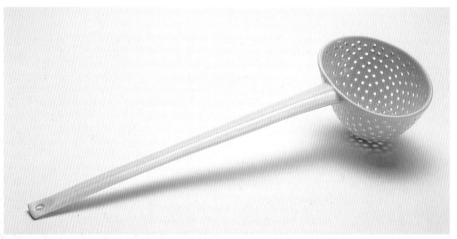

White Sieve, Pierced | 2006 ▶

7 x 6 x 5 inches (17.8 x 15.2 x 12.7 cm)
Hand-thrown porcelain; fired on rim, gas
fired in reduction, cone 12; calcium glaze
Photo by Terence Bogue

▲ Pair of Oval Dishes with Handles | 1996

Left: 5¾ x 3½ x 2¾ inches (14.6 x 8.9 x 7 cm);
right: 6¾ x 4 ½ x 4¼ inches (17.1 x 11.4 x 10.8 cm)
Hand-thrown and altered porcelain, new base added; blue
underglaze decoration; reduction fired; gas kiln, cone 12
Photo by Terence Bogue

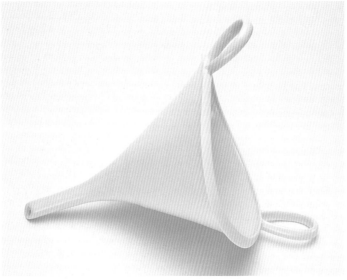

◀ **Yellow and White Funnel, Pierced** │ 2006

9 x 7 x 5¾ inches (22.9 x 17.8 x 14.6 cm)
Hand-thrown and altered porcelain, constructed;
pierced; fired on rim, gas fired in reduction, cone 12;
calcium glaze
Photos by Terence Bogue

▲ **White Sieve, Pierced; Black Ladle, Pierced** │ 2006

Sieve: 9 x 7½ x 4 ¾ inches (22.9 x 19 x 12 cm);
ladle: 4 x 3¼ x 14½ inches (10.2 x 8.3 x 36.8 cm)
Hand-thrown porcelain, pierced; fired on rim, gas fired in
reduction, cone 12; calcium glaze
Photo by Terence Bogue

▲ **Pair of Oval Jugs** | 1996

Left: 3¼ x 6¼ x 3¼ inches (8.3 x 15.9 x 8.3 cm); right: 3¼ x 6 x 3½ inches (8.3 x 15.2 x 8.9 cm) Hand-thrown and altered porcelain, new base added; blue underglaze decoration; reduction fired; gas kiln, cone 12
Photos by Terence Bogue

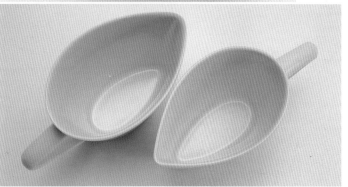

Black Oval Dish, White Spoon, Black Oval Jug | 2003 ▶

Group: 4 x 14¼ x 6 inches
(10.2 x 36.2 x 15.2 cm)
Hand-thrown and altered porcelain,
new base added; gas fired in reduction,
cone 12; calcium glaze
Photo by Terence Bogue

◀ **White Bowl and Ladle, Pierced** | 2005

Bowl: 4¼ x 9½ x 9½ inches
(10.8 x 24.1 x 24.1 cm);
ladle: 3¾ x 2¾ x 10¼ inches
(9.5 x 7 x 26 cm)
Hand-thrown porcelain; pierced; calcium glaze
gas fired in reduction, cone 12
Photo by Terence Bogue

" When the shroud of surface decoration fell away, my attention turned more strongly toward the exploration of new questions, of subtle issues: of relationships between forms and surfaces, of light falling on edges, of space and mood. "

▲ Oval Dish and Scoop, Pierced | 2005

Dish: 7 x 9¾ x 9¾ inches (17.8 x 24.8 x 24.8 cm);
scoop: 6 x 10¾ x 6½ inches (15.2 x 27.3 x 16.5 cm)
Hand-thrown and altered porcelain, new base added;
gas fired in reduction, cone 12; calcium glaze
Photo by Terence Bogue

Arne Åse

DESPITE HAVING MOVED through a number of styles and techniques over the years, Arne Åse's work has always combined crispness of form with a lyrical surface. Staccato patterns combine with abstract flowing forms in a jazz-like fusion of brushwork on white clay. Åse's most recent work often features compositions of pure white on white, using the natural translucence of the delicately thin, unglazed fine white porcelain to allow light to amplify his brushwork. The result is a complex melding of images, abstract yet closely referencing natural forms: shadows, leaves, nets, and landscape.

Ever the innovator, Åse developed casting slips including acrylic medium to cast very thin (2-mm thickness) slabs of porcelain. These slabs are strong but flexible when unfired, making it possible for Åse to cast them much larger than otherwise possible and work with them without breaking the paper-thin clay.

▲ **Porcelain Painting and Etching on a Bowl** | 2000
11¾ x 11¾ inches (30 x 30 cm)
Wheel-thrown porcelain; "etched," brush-painted, painted resist, colored with soluble salts; unglazed; electric fired (in Kanthal Super) with gas injection for reduction, 2336°F (1280°C)
Photo by Glenn Hagebru

▲ **Untitled,** | 2006

9⅞ x 3⅛ inches (25 x 8 cm)
Wheel-thrown porcelain; "etched", brush-painted, painted resist,
colored with soluble salts; unglazed; Kanthal super, gas reduction in
electric kiln, 2336°F (1280°C)
Photo by Jo Åse

▲ **Untitled** | 1988

7⅛ x 9 inches (18 x 23 cm)
Wheel-thrown porcelain; clay inlay and etching;
unglazed; electric fired (in Kanthal Super) with
gas injection for reduction, 2336°F (1280°C)
Photo by Glenn Hagebru, Arne Åse, and Jo Åse

Untitled | 1986 ▶

7⅞ x 9 ⅞ inches (20 x 25 cm)
Wheel-thrown porcelain; clay inlay; unglazed;
electric fired (in Kanthal Super) with gas
injection for reduction, 2336°F (1280°C)
Photo by Glenn Hagebru

"I decided to use the most traditional object in ceramic art as a canvas. I am insisting that a bowl can be considered art in the same way that a sculpture can. My challenge was to create artistic expressions combining me, the bowl, and the brush."

▲ **Untitled** │ 1989

55 x 55 inches (140 x 140 cm)
Unglazed porcelain; reduction fired,
2318°F–2336°F (1270°C –1280°C)
Photo by artist

"Technique has a rather low status in parts of the art world. But technology, combined with hearts and thoughts, creates all developments and changes in artistic expression. Ideas create the need for tools, and tools create the need for ideas."

▲ Untitled | 1987
4¼ x 3⅛ inches (11 x 8 cm)
Unglazed porcelain; water-color painted; reduction fired, 2318°F–2336°F (1270°C–1280°C)
Photo by Roar Hoyland

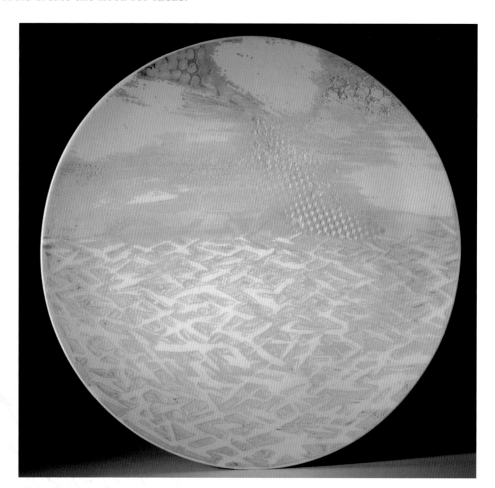

▲ Untitled | 1993
2 x 23⅝ inches (5 x 60 cm)
Unglazed porcelain; "etched" and watercolor painted; reduction fired, 2318°F–2336°F (1270°C–1280°C)
Photo by Glenn Hagebru

▲ **Untitled** │ 1993

    7⅞ x 7 inches (20 x 18 cm)
    Unglazed porcelain; "etched"; reduction fired,
    2318°F–2336°F (1270°C–1280°C)
    Photo by Glenn Hagebru

◀ **Untitled** │ 1994

    31½ x 19¾ inches (80 x 50 cm)
    Unglazed porcelain; "etched" and
    watercolor painted; reduction fired,
    2318°F–2336°F (1270°C–1280°C)
    Photo by Georg Parmann

ARNE ÅSE

▲ **Untitled** │ 1994

2 x 23⅝ inches (5 x 60 cm)
Unglazed porcelain; etched and watercolor painted;
reduction fired, cone 2318°F–2336°F (1270°C–1280°C)
Photo by Glenn Hagebru

"I have functioned like a jazz musician, an
improviser. I like to think that an artist has
impatience in his mind that always forces him
look for new solutions in his creative project.**"**

▲ **Untitled** | 2006

4 x 11¾ inches (10 x 30 cm)
Unglazed porcelain; etched and
watercolor painted; reduction fired,
2318°F–2336°F (1270°C–1280°C)
Photo by Jo Åse

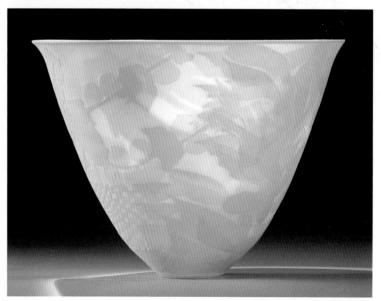

Untitled | 1994 ▶

9⅞ x 7⅞ inches (25 x 20 cm)
Wheel-thrown porcelain; etching,
brush-painted; unglazed; electric fired
(in Kanthal Super) with gas injection for
reduction, 2336°F (1280°C)
Photo by Glenn Hagebru

ARNE ÅSE

Sandra Black

THE DELICATE CARVING and piercing in Sanda Black's porcelain bowls create sensuously luminous forms: plant images wrap around some of the forms, geometric shapes dance up the sides of others. Her work always has a crispness and formal elegance that frame the images created by the rhythmically pierced shapes covering the surface of her work, reflecting Black's various concerns with environmental issues in her native Australia.

▲ **Growth Series** │ 2005

6 x 10½ inches (15.2 x 26.7 cm)
Seeley's Lady White porcelain casting slip;
carved, pierced, polished; unglazed; electric
fired, cone 7
Photo by Victor France

"In the early 1970s, having always worked with very gritty earthenware and stoneware, I first found porcelain rather unpleasant to the touch. Yet I persisted and kept the very first piece I made: a small, molded coil dish."

◄ Group of Geometric
Porcelain Vessels | 2001

Largest: 6 x 8¼ inches (15.2 x 21 cm);
smallest: 2½ x 5½ inches (6.4 x 14 cm)
Seeley's Lady White and Ebony porcelain
casting slips; carved, pierced; unglazed;
electric fired, cone 7
Photo by Victor France

"From a period of
learning about slip
casting and making
bone china emerged
several series that
drew inspiration from
elements of classicism,
Asian cultural artifacts,
and allusions to film
and architecture in
order to express the
grief process."

Time Well Series | 1989 ▶

28½ x 8¾ inches (72.4 x 22.2 cm)
Thrown and slip cast bone china
and JB1 porcelain; assembled;
wrapped with slip-impregnated
fabrics, foam, airbrushed stained
slips; unglazed; electric fired,
cone 8
Photo by Haru Sameshima

▲ Rites of Passage III | 1988

25½ x 9½ inches (64.8 x 24.1 cm)
Thrown and slip cast Kusnik bone china,
JB1 porcelain; assembled; wrapped with
slip-impregnated fabrics, foam, barbed
wire, airbrushed color slips; unglazed;
electric fired, cone 8
Photo by Haru Sameshima
Collection of the Auckland Museum and Art Gallery

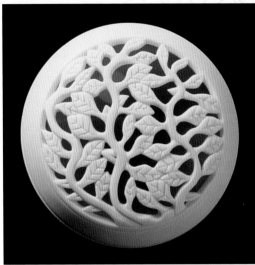
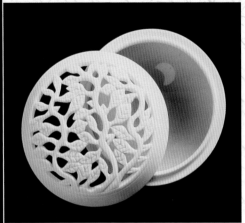

▲ **Tropical Vine Box Daintree**
Series II │ 2000

1¾ x 3¼ inches (4.4 x 8.3 cm)
Wheel-thrown Southern Ice porcelain;
carved, polished; matte glazed interior;
electric fired, cone 10
Photos by Victor France

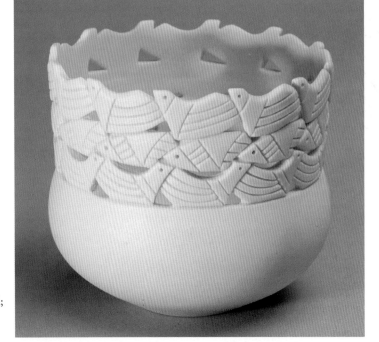

Geometric Bird and Fish Bowl │ 1993 ▶

2¾ x 3¼ inches (7 x 8.3 cm)
Wheel-thrown JB1 porcelain; carved, polished;
unglazed; electric fired, cone 10
Photo by Victor France

▲ **Two Triangular Vessels** | 1992

Left: 8¾ x 3¼ inches (22.2 x 8.3 cm); right: ½ x 3¼ inches (8.9 x 8.3 cm)
Slip cast Seeley's Lady White porcelain; carved, pieced, polished; unglazed; electric fired, cone 7
Photo by Victor France

◀ Deco Vase Series │ 1992

2¾ x 2½ inches (7 x 6.4 cm)
Wheel-thrown JB1 porcelain; carved;
unglazed; electric fired, cone 10
Photo by Victor France

Curved Geometric Vessel │ 2002 ▶

2¾ x 5½ inches (7 x 14 cm)
Seeley's Ebony porcelain casting slips;
carved, pierced; unglazed; electric
fired, cone 7
Photo by Victor France

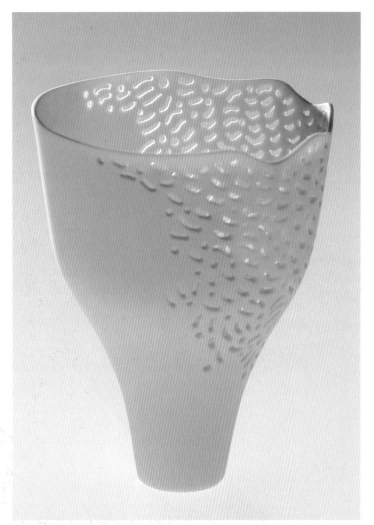

▲ **Palm Box–Daintree Series II** | 2000

1¾ x 3¼ inches (4.4 x 8.3 cm)
Wheel-thrown Southern Ice porcelain; carved,
polished; matte glazed interior; electric fired,
cone 10
Photo by Steve Nebauer

◀ **Small Pierced Vessel** | 1985

3 x 2 inches (7.6 x 5.1 cm)
Westwood porcelain casting slip; pierced, polished;
unglazed; electric fired, cone 6
Photo by Leon Bird

"Porcelain as a medium offers many challenges. Each clay body behaves differently and each shape brings its own set of issues to solve. These very qualities, along with porcelain's whiteness and translucency, are what give such satisfaction to the process."

▲ **Growth Series 7 Vines Vessel** | 2006

6 x 10¼ inches (15.2 x 26 cm)
Seeley's Lady White porcelain casting slip; carved, pierced, polished; unglazed; electric fired, cone 7
Photo by Victor France

CHUNG

Sam Chung

RESONATING WITH elements of classic Chinese and Korean porcelain, Sam Chung's teapots and vases also represent aspects of contemporary form and aesthetics. The readily apparent architectural quality of Chung's analytical constructions adds greatly to their appeal. Such contrasts make for a potent mix. His complex thrown and hand-built forms, with their sensuous curves, crisply defined edges, and often lively dotted surfaces, all combine in elegant and superbly functional pots.

Ewer | 2003 ▶

6 x 5 x 5 inches (15.2 x 12.7 x 12.7 cm)
Slab-built porcelain; satin red glaze;
soda fired, cone 10
Photo by artist

Ewer | 2006 ▶

6 x 5 x 3 inches
(15.2 x 12.7 x 7.6 cm)
Slab-built porcelain;
satin matte glaze;
soda fired, cone 10
Photo by artist

▲ **Ewer** | 2004

    6 x 5 x 3 inches (15.2 x 12.7 x 7.6 cm)
    Slab-built porcelain; matte black glaze; soda fired, cone 10
    Photo by artist

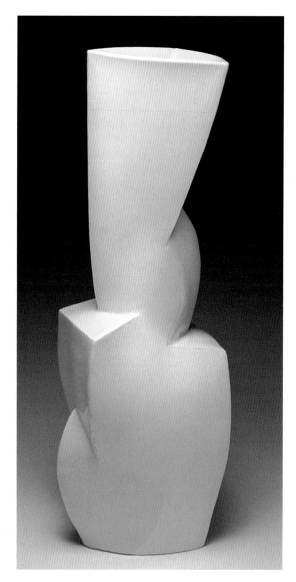

▲ **Vase** | 2005

    15 x 5 x 4 inches (38.1 x 12.7 x 10.2 cm)
    Slab-built porcelain; raw clay, celadon;
    gas fired in reduction, cone 10
    Photo by artist

"The elegance and formality of Chinese and Korean pots—particularly those from the Song and Koryo dynasties—first inspired me to use porcelain to emphasize the idea of preciousness, to articulate fine details in my forms, and to showcase purity in glaze colors.**"**

▲ Pitcher | 2004

12 x 8 x 5 inches (30.5 x 20.3 x 12.7 cm)
Slab-built porcelain; satin yellow glaze; soda fired, cone 10
Photo by artist

SAM CHUNG

▲ Pitcher | 2006

12 x 7 x 5 inches (30.5 x 17.8 x 12.7 cm)
Slab-built porcelain; satin red glaze; soda fired, cone 10
Photo by artist

▲ Pitcher | 2003

12 x 6 x 5 inches (30.5 x 15.2 x 12.7 cm)
Slab-built porcelain; matte black glaze; soda fired, cone 10
Photo by artist

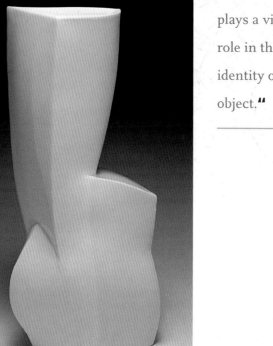

"I had the good fortune of learning how to make pots in Minnesota, which has a rich pottery-making tradition. My first ceramics teachers were all affected by the aesthetic of the Japanese Mingei folk pottery movement, and I became fascinated with the notion of how function plays a vital role in the identity of an object."

▲ **Vase** | 2005

13 x 6 x 4 inches (33 x 15.2 x 10.2 cm)
Slab-built porcelain; raw clay, celadon;
gas fired in reduction, cone 10
Photos by artist

SAM CHUNG

"Wherever I go, my attention is drawn to buildings and structures in their environment—everything from industrial factories to dilapidated barns. Orchestrating collaborations between form, space, function, and design is both demanding and exciting.**"**

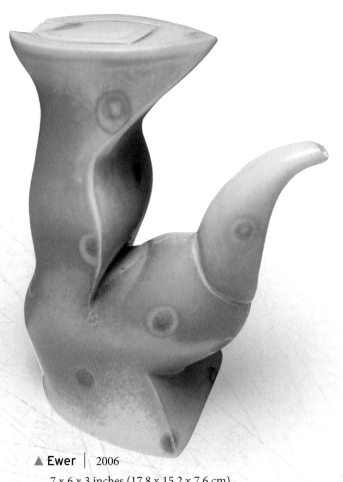

▲ **Ewer** | 2006
7 x 6 x 3 inches (17.8 x 15.2 x 7.6 cm)
Slab-built porcelain; satin red glaze;
soda fired, cone 10
Photo by artist

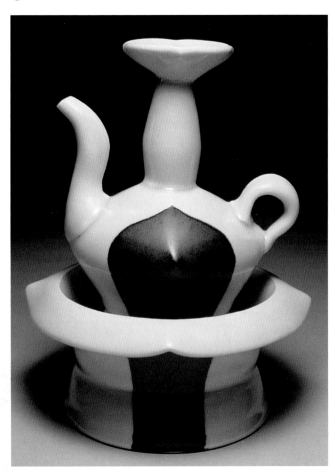

▲ **Ewer with Stand** | 1997
7 x 6 x 6 inches (17.8 x 15.2 x 15.2 cm)
Wheel-thrown and altered porcelain; celadon and matte
black glazes; gas fired in reduction, cone 10
Photo by artist

◀ **Teapot** | 2003

6 x 8 x 4 inches (15.2 x 20.3 x 10.2 cm)
Slab-built porcelain; satin matte glaze;
soda fired, cone 10
Photo by artist

Teapot | 2006 ▶

6 x 7 x 4 inches (15.2 x 17.8 x 10.2 cm)
Slab-built porcelain; satin white and
apple green celadon glaze; gas fired in
oxidation, cone 10
Photo by artist

SAM CHUNG

Diane Kenney

THE FUNCTIONAL, wood-fired, and nature-inspired porcelain by Dianne Kenney has a comfortable feel, a user-friendly scale, and a warmth from the wood-ash glaze that makes it glow. Beautifully proportioned, her work demands to be used and handled. It's clear that she intimately understands what the wood-firing process offers to her work. She sets up the edges, textures, surfaces, and forms of her porcelain ware to be highly receptive and reactive to the firing process. Pieces such as her Etched Jar are enlivened by inscribed marks through orange-colored flashing slip, revealing the whiteness of the porcelain beneath.

◀ **Large Covered Jar** | 2003

12 x 9 x 10 inches (30.5 x 23 x 25.5 cm)
Wheel-thrown porcelain (in two sections); slipped on bottom; glazed lid and collar; soda and salt fired, cone 10
Photo by Sanjay Jani, Akar Design

▲ **Covered Jars** | 1996

12 x 6½ x 10 inches (30.5 x 16.5 x 25.5 cm)

Wheel-thrown porcelain, accessorized; partially slipped, partially glazed with shino; wood fired in
Bourry box kiln, cone 10

Photo by artist

"I look for beauty, generosity, rightness of proportion, and exciting surfaces with elements of surprise in my work. I am very happy when someone tells me they drink out of one of my cups every day."

▲ **Cups and Saucers** | 2005

Cups: 3½ x 3½ x 3 inches
(9 x 9 x 7.5 cm);
saucers: 5 inches (12.5 cm)
in diameter
Wheel-thrown porcelain; glaze;
soda and salt fired, cone 10
Photo by artist

◀ **Oval Serving Dish** | 2006

4 x 8 x 7 inches
(10 x 20.5 x 18 cm)
Wheel-thrown and altered
porcelain; slipped exterior, glazed
interior; soda and salt fired,
cone 10
Photo by artist

▲ **Covered Jar** │ 2003

10½ x 9 x 9 inches (26.7 x 23 x 23 cm)
Wheel-thrown porcelain; glaze; soda and
salt fired, cone 10
Photo by artist

▲ **Ewer with Removable Top** │ 1999

9 x 6 x 8½ inches (23 x 15 x 21.5 cm)
Wheel-thrown and altered porcelain; slipped
exterior, ash melting furnace; wood fired in
Bourry box kiln, cone 10
Photo by artist

▲ **Etched Jar** | 2006

6 x 5½ x 4 inches (15 x 14 x 10 cm)
Wheel-thrown porcelain; slipped and etched exterior;
soda and salt fired, cone 10
Photo by artist

▲ **Ruffly, Dotted, Sugar Jar** | 2003

5½ x 6 x 5 inches (14 x 15 x 12.5 cm)
Wheel-thrown porcelain; etched; amber
glaze; soda and salt fired, cone 10
Photo by Sanjay Jani, Akar Design Gallery

"Each piece leads me to the next one—a never-ending, insatiable process of learning, seeing, and making, always with respect for the material, paying attention to what each new lump of clay can do and be and teach."

▲ **Teapot Set** | 2006

    Teapot: 5½ x 7½ x 4½ inches (14 x 19 x 11.5 cm)
    Wheel-thrown porcelain; applied spout, pulled handle; glazed lids and shoulder;
    slip on exterior of cups and teapot bottom; wood fired, cone 10
    Photos by artist

DIANE KENNEY

"There are quiet moments in the studio when I am completely focused, with the music just right or just silence. In those moments I really connect with the material and move it around with ease and some daring, and I see and feel myself creating from my heart and nothing else matters. I live for those moments.**"**

◀ Etched Jar | 2003

10 x 9 x 9 ½ inches (25.5 x 23 x 24 cm)
Wheel-thrown porcelain; slipped,
carved; soda and salt fired, cone 10
Photo by artist

DIANE KENNEY

▲ Covered Jar │ 1996

    12 x 7 x 10½ inches (30.5 x 18 x 26.5 cm)
Wheel-thrown porcelain; slipped on bottom
two-thirds; shino glaze on top section and lid;
wood fired in Bourry box kiln, cone 10
Photo by artist

▲ Lusty Jar │ 2006

    9 x 5 x 6½ inches (23 x 12.5 x 16.5 cm)
Wheel-thrown porcelain; slipped on
bottom section; glaze; soda and salt
fired, cone 10
Photo by artist

DIANE KENNEY

About the Curator

In 1970, Richard Burkett began his 35-year career in pottery by throwing ashtrays for the late Indiana potter Richard Peeler. Burkett founded Wild Rose Pottery in 1973 and created salt-glazed pottery for ten years. He now works with a wide range of ceramic materials, including porcelain, functional stoneware, and mixed media sculpture. Burkett has an MFA in both ceramics and photography, and is a Professor of Art at San Diego State University. He is the co-author of *Ceramics: A Potter's Handbook* and created Hyperglaze, a popular glaze calculation software program. Burkett plays bluegrass with his band, Gone Tomorrow, as often as possible.

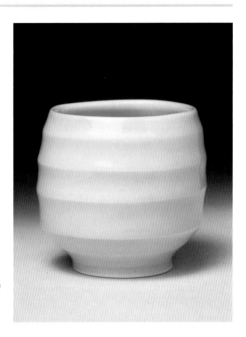

Teabowl | 2007 ▶
4 x 4 x 4 inches (10.2 x 10.2 x 10.2 cm)
Translucent porcelain, celadon glaze
Photo by artist

Acknowledgments

The talented artists who agreed to contribute work to this book deserve tremendous thanks, both for their beautiful work and for the fact that they took time from their creative endeavors, gathered some images, and even jotted a few thoughts about what makes them tick. Grateful appreciate, too, to Richard Burkett, who guided us in the selection of this stellar roster and made astute observations on the nature of each artist's work. In particular we want to acknowledge the assistance of Mr. Tashimoyo.

Bringing together all the parts of this book demanded more than a little from the Lark staff, too. Shannon Quinn-Tucker made superhuman effort to acquire and organize every last image, word, and credit. She was ably assisted in editorial matters by Mark Bloom and Cassie Moore. Finally, the stunning design you see here belongs to Kristi Pfeffer, who exhibited total sangfroid during the long design process. You guys rock.

Artists' Biographies

Arne Åse

Åse's technique of using watercolor on porcelain—emulated by other porcelain artists—has been analyzed in national magazines such as *Studio Potter*, *Ceramics Today*, and *ClayArt*. His original plan, however, was to study architecture (ceramics was his second choice). In the mid-to-late 1960s, he created abstract expressionist pieces in rough clay, but he felt the clay compromised his vision. He shifted to porcelain, which has allowed him to better express his own identity. Born in Norway, Åse has been a ceramics professor at the National Academy of Art and Design in Oslo, Norway, since 1987.

Susan Beiner

Strongly influenced by the rich tradition of the European porcelain manufacturers, Beiner felt particularly drawn to the 17th- and 18th-century pieces made by Meissen and Sèvres. Recognition for her work came in 2002, when the National Council on Education for the Ceramic Arts (NCECA) recognized her as an emerging artist. Her work has since been shown worldwide, from The Los Angeles County Museum of Art in California to the Yixing Ceramics Museum in Yixing, China. She's currently the head of the ceramic department at California State University.

Curtis Benzle

Benzle studied and served an apprenticeship under U.S. master potter Robert Eckels. In 2000 and 2001, Benzle participated in Japan's prestigious Seto Residency Program, where he worked with Japanese "New Bone" porcelain, developed a unique method of making and firing pieces in individual saggers, and studied the nericomi technique, which employs the use of colored clay and slip. Now he teaches at the Columbus College of Art and Design in Ohio and also owns Benzle Applied Arts, a company that makes porcelain lighting and accessories.

Sandra Black

Black began working with porcelain in 1975, and like all artists, her style has evolved since then. She now uses simple forms to enhance her elaborate surface treatments. A founding member of the Ceramic Arts Association of Western Australia, she has participated in over 160 invitational and juried exhibitions. She's also held 30 solo exhibitions. Black began with an Associateship in Art Teaching at the Western Australia Institute of Technology at Curtin University, and was later awarded the 19th National Craft Acquisition Award by the Museum and Art Gallery of Northern Territory, Australia.

Sam Chung

Inspired by the visual and tactile nature of the pottery of the Goryeo Dynasty in Korea and the Song Dynasty of China, Chung makes pots that reflect refined elegance on a small scale, where beauty is found in utility. His work can be found in several permanent collections, including the Jingdezhen Ceramic Institute, Jingdezhen, China. After 20 years as an Associate Professor of Ceramics at the Northern Michigan University School of Art and Design, Chung recently accepted the position of Assistant Professor of Ceramics at Herberger College of the Arts, Arizona State University.

Philip Cornelius

Cornelius developed a signature "thinware" porcelain, which he has produced since the 1970s. While the porcelain is ultra-thin and appears almost breakable, it's actually quite sturdy. He has twice been awarded a fellowship through the National Endowment for the Arts, and his work is part of the permanent collection of the Smithsonian Institute, Washington, D.C. Cornelius earned a Master of Fine Arts degree from Claremont Graduate University, Claremont, California, where he worked with Paul Soldner.

Claire Curneen

One of the leading ceramics artists currently working in Europe, Curneen creates work that often highlights religious figures, such as her studies of St. Sebastian. She hand-rolls small porcelain pieces and joins her figures together beginning at the feet. Her work has been exhibited throughout the world and is held in many of the world's major ceramic collections, including the National Museum Wales and Victoria and Albert Museum, London, England. Curneen studied at Crawford College of Art and Design in Cork, Ireland, before earning a post-graduate diploma at the University of Ulster, Belfast.

Janet DeBoos

DeBoos has written two best-selling books—*Glazes for Australian Potters* and *More Glazes for Australian Potters*—and has co-authored *Handbook for Australian Potters*. She completed training in ceramics at East Sydney National Art School in 1971 after earning a degree in science. She is currently Head of Ceramics at the Australian National University School of Art.

Edmund De Waal

It's no surprise that De Waal's work explores the relationship between contemporary studio ceramic practice and the historical canon. When only 16 years old, he was apprenticed within the Leach tradition of Anglo-Oriental pottery for three years. He has since worked in both Britain and Japan making Leach-inspired pottery. His work can be found in many renowned public collections, such as the Museum of Arts and Design, New York, and the Los Angeles County Museum of Art. De Waal is Professor of Ceramics at the University of Westminster, London, England.

Paul Dresang

An internationally recognized artist, Dresang is best known for creating distinctive yet functional wheel-thrown pottery, as well as ceramic sculptural constructions known as trompe l'oeil, which literally translates into "fool the eye." Public collections such as the Smithsonian Museum, Renwick Gallery, Washington, D.C., and the Mint Museum of Craft and Design, Charlotte, North Carolina, hold his work. Dresang received a Master of Fine Arts degree from the University of Minnesota in 1974.

Ruth Duckworth

Duckworth is internationally known as one of the leading figures in ceramic arts. In a career spanning more than six decades that follows her personal journey—fleeing from Nazi Germany to England at the outset of World War II, and settling in the United States in the mid-1960s—Duckworth has created an immense and important body of work and played an important role in the continuation of the modernist tradition. Duckworth currently lives and works in Chicago, Illinois.

Edward Eberle

Eberle is known for his line drawings in black terra sigillata on matte white porcelain. He exhibits regularly with several prestigious galleries, including the Garth Clark Gallery, New York, and Perimeter Gallery, Chicago. He has earned the National Endowment for the Arts Grant in 1987 and the Pennsylvania Council on the Arts Grant in 1986, 1989, and 1992. Eberle earned his Masters of Fine Arts from the New York State College of Ceramics, Alfred University, in 1972.

Silvie Granatelli

Granatelli's pottery is about the presentation of food. In crafting her pieces, she explores the rituals, mood, and atmosphere of tableware in various cultures and societies. Her work has been published in numerous ceramics publications. She earned a Master of Fine Arts degree from Montana State University in 1975 and now conducts ceramics workshops around the country.

Gwyn Hanssen Pigott

An Australian artist, Hanssen Pigott is recognized worldwide for her minimalistic still life groupings of porcelain vessels. Her work has been exhibited in Taiwan, New York, and Munich. She was presented with a Visual Arts and Crafts Emeritus award in 1997 and an Australia Council Fellowship in 1998.

Rebecca Harvey

Harvey says her work "owes an incredible debt to the English majolica of the mid- to late-1800s. She and her work has been featured in *Ceramic Review* and *ClayArt* magazines. She earned her Masters of Fine Arts in Ceramics from Cranbrook Academy of Art, Bloomfield Hills, Michigan, and she's now an assistant professor in the Department of Art's Ceramics program at Ohio State University.

Nicholas Homoky

Homoky's work is mainly centered on the porcelain vessel. He co-authored a book about his techniques titled *Nicholas Homoky*. Born in Hungary, he currently resides in Bristol, England. In fact, he earned his Bachelor of Arts degree from the University of West England in Bristol and completed his Master of Fine Arts at the Royal College of Art in London.

Harlan House

Since graduating from the Alberta College of Art in 1969, House has worked as a potter, maintaining a successful studio practice in the village of Lonsdale, Ontario. He has had over 70 solo exhibitions since 1968, indicating a lifelong obsession with the craft. House was born in Vancouver, British Columbia, Canada.

Sergei Isupov

Isupov has been a featured artist in many Lark books, in ceramics and fine craft periodicals, and in solo and group exhibitions, including numerous times in the bi-annual Sculptural Objects Functional Art (SOFA) exhibitions. He received his art education at the Ukrainian State Art School and at the Art Institute of Tallinn, Estonia, where he earned his Bachelor of Arts and Master of Fine Arts degrees.

Suk-Young Kang

Kang is considered the pioneer of using the slip-casting technique in modern Korean ceramics. In 2004, he built a gigantic installation for the Summer Olympics in Greece. A modified version of it is displayed in the Seoul Museum of Art. He is currently a professor in the Department of Ceramic Art at Ewha Womans University in Seoul, Korea.

Diane Kenney

Diane Kenney has been working as a potter and pottery teacher for close to 30 years. Functional clay pots have always been her primary focus. The founding director of the Carbondale Clay Center, she currently resides in Western Colorado.

Kim Soo-Jeong

Kim's aim in her work is to express the energy of a lotus flower in a variety of ways. By all accounts, she has succeeded. She has been a juror multiple times at the Korean Crafts Exhibition and has participated in numerous national and international shows. Kim is a professor in the Ceramics Department at Ewha Womans University, which is where she earned her Master of Arts degree.

Yikyung Kim

Kim is one of the best-known contemporary Korean ceramists. An important theme in her work is Confucianist rituals, in which ceramic objects play an important role. For this reason, she designs the "feet" of her objects with care. Objects with a "high foot" play a role in ancestor worship, while those with a "low foot" are meant for daily use.

Taizo Kuroda

Born in Japan, Kuroda studied ceramics in Quebec, New York, and Paris, before building a studio in Futo, on the Izu Peninsula of the Japanese island of Honsh-u. In 1992, he developed his signature white porcelain, which has been exhibited around the globe. Several articles have been written about Kuroda's technique, which differs from many other porcelain artists in that he uses either a non-sparkling glaze or no glaze at all.

Les Lawrence

As a ceramic artist, Lawrence has become known for his use of screen-printing decals and for his sculptural teapots. He has exhibited in over 160 national and international exhibitions and has served as co-chair of the National Council on Education for the Ceramic Arts. Born in Corpus Christi, Texas, he now lives and works in San Diego, California.

Leah Leitson

Leitson's forms are predominately inspired by two distinct sources: plant forms found in nature and the 18th- and 19th-century decorative arts, particularly utilitarian silver tableware and Sèvres porcelain. A member of the Piedmont Craftsmen, Inc., and the Southern Highland Craft Guild, she is a studio potter who lives and works in Asheville, North Carolina. She holds a BFA from New York State College of Ceramics, Alfred University, and an MFA in ceramics from Louisiana State University.

Ann Linnemann

Linnemann makes sculptural forms that embody elements of human movement and body language. Her work has been shown all over the world, including the Galerie Carlin in Paris and the American Crafts Museum in New York City. Since 2001, she has been the director of the International Ceramic Research Center in Denmark.

Bodil Manz

For many years now, Manz has been known as a master of eggshell porcelain. In addition to her slip cast porcelain cylinders, Manz also designs tea and dinner sets, and has even made large-scale architectural pieces. Her work is represented in the National Museum of Sweden, the Danish Museum of Decorative Art, and the Victoria and Albert Museum. Manz was born in Copenhagen, Denmark.

Andrew Martin

After visiting Greece and Turkey, Martin was inspired by the Minoan pots of Crete and the Iznik tiles of Istanbul. He has earned many honors since, including two Fellowship Grants from the National Endowment for the Arts. Martin earned his Bachelor of Fine Arts degree from the Kansas City Art Institute and his Master of Fine Arts from Alfred University. He resides in Los Angeles, California.

Paul Mathieu

Mathieu is the author of *Sex Pots*, a book that explores the influence of sex and sexuality in pottery from the past to the present day. He was a recipient of the 2000 Jean A. Chalmers Award for Excellence in Crafts. He currently teaches at the Emily Carr Institute of Art + Design + Media.

Matthew Metz

Metz's work is influenced by various sources, including Asian pottery, Greek and Roman pots, early American decorative arts, face jugs, and other folk traditions. His carved and drawn surfaces function decoratively as well as practically in everyday life. In 1990, Metz was a recipient of the National Endowment for the Arts fellowship. He lives in Houston, Minnesota, where he is a full-time potter.

Keisuke Mizuno

Born in Japan, Mizuno came to the United States to study other subjects and discovered ceramics in college. All of the transitions of life, from the embryonic stage to death and decay, are present in his work. His intimate and intricate porcelain pieces often use flowers and fruit as an essential element, a starting point for Mizuno's reflections on the transience of existence. His work is represented in the Museum of Arts and Design in New York and The Renwick Gallery of The National Museum of American Art, Smithsonian Institute in Washington, DC

Aysha Peltz

Peltz attempts to build landscape and terrain in the imagined space of her pots. While she enjoys working in a larger scale, her pots convey a sense of directness, which is a quality that she facilitates in her ceramic process. In 2005, she was awarded an Emerging Artist Award at the National Council on Education for the Ceramic Arts (NCECA), and her work was selected for exhibition in its prestigious bi-annual Clay National show. A studio potter, she lives and works in Whitingham, Vermont.

Ilona Romule

Romule is internationally recognized for her slip cast, gothic-inspired porcelain figures, and for her use of semi-erotic imagery. She received an honorable mention at the First World Ceramic Biennale, Icheon, Kyonngi Province, Korea, and participated in the International Storytelling Ceramics Symposium in Guldagergaard, Denmark. A featured artist at the Guldagergaard Ceramic Research Center in Skælskør, Denmark, Romule received her Master of Fine Arts degree from the Latvian Art Academy.

Richard Shaw

With his perfectly cast porcelain objects and overglaze transfer decals, Shaw is the master of trompe l'oeil sculpture. His work captures the commonplace, the poetic, and the surreal with the sensibility of a comedian. Coming out of the San Francisco Bay area in the late 1960s, he has long been affiliated with the Funk movement. Shaw's work is represented in the Addison Gallery of American Art in Andover, at Arizona State University, The Contemporary Museum in Honolulu, and the National Museum of Modern Art, Tokyo, among others.

Linda Sikora

Jars and teapots are the main focus of Sikora's current work, and she concerns herself with the specific engineering particular to function. She curated "Old World, New World" at the La Coste Gallery in Massachusetts, and participated in invitationals in China, Korea, and Japan. Sikora is an Assistant Professor of Ceramic Art in the New York State College of Ceramics at Alfred University's School of Art & Design, but she spends her summers in Minnesota.

Christopher P. Staley

Staley once wrote an article entitled, "How a Handmade Cup Can Save the World." His pots now reside in major museums, as well as in friends' cupboards. The major collections that hold his works include the Los Angeles County Museum of Art, the Smithsonian's Renwick Gallery, and the Victoria & Albert Museum in London. Staley is a professor of Ceramic Arts at Penn(sylvania) State University. He was awarded the Graduate Faculty Teaching Award in 2007.

Piet Stockmans

Stockmans is a Belgian ceramist and designer who has limited his palette to a white porcelain in combination with a blue slip; however, this has not limited his prolific output nor his creativity. From 1966 to 1989, Stockmans worked with the Dutch company Royal Mosa, where he designed the world's most ubiquitous coffee cup, titled "Sonja." He resides in Belgium, but has had exhibitions in Paris, Amsterdam, Helsinki, and New York.

Prue Venables

After receiving a science degree at Melbourne University, Venables left for England in the late 1970s to become a professional flute player. Somewhere along the way, she became sidetracked and returned to Australia thirteen years later as a highly accomplished potter. Venables has drawn much of her inspiration from the elegance and restraint of the 18th- and 19th-century English potters.

Kurt Weiser

After a stint as Director of the Archie Bray Foundation in Helena, Montana, Weiser started teaching ceramics at Arizona State University in 2000, where he has held the position of Regents' Professor of Art ever since. While Arizona is his home now, he was born in Lansing, Michigan.

Sunkoo Yuh

Yuh was awarded both the Joan Mitchell Foundation Grant and a University of Georgia Faculty Research Grant in 2005. His work can be seen in the permanent collection of The Renwick Gallery at the Smithsonian Institute, as well as many other public and private collections around the world. Yuh teaches at the University of Georgia and at the Penland School of Crafts in North Carolina. He earned his Bachelor of Fine Arts from Hong-Ik University, in Seoul, Korea, and a Masters of Fine Arts from New York State College of Ceramics, Alfred University.

Artist Index